D0850936

YOUR NAME

HOW TO BUILD AND REPAIR
YOUR REPUTATION AT ANY AGE

MIKE SIVER
MAC, CDVC, BCBC

PUBLISHED BY FIDELI PUBLISHING, INC.

Start Your New Direction Today

YOUR NAME

HOW TO BUILD AND REPAIR
YOUR REPUTATION AT ANY AGE

Table of Contents

PROTECTING YOUR NAME FROM OUTSIDE INFLUENCES

DAMAGE CONTROL

Foreword

The basic requirement for being sure you take care of something and make it excellent is to value it. It's the difference between the car the privileged kid was given that's dirty and beat up and the spotless, well-cared for car that was earned by the kid next door. Who do you think values the car more?

Value is a fundamental element in an individual's or group's success. Every dedicated member of a football team, every soldier in any branch of the service, every revered family member, etc. all have pride in the fundamental element of their existence, of who they are.

I recall just how well this point was driven home for me. When I was 18 years old and home on leave before going to Vietnam, one of my parent's friends asked which branch of the military I was serving in. I remember answering with an almost apologetic tone, "The Marines." Now, I wasn't ashamed — I just didn't want to rub it in because there were lots of folks that weren't Marines and I didn't want to brag and hurt their feelings. I believed just uttering the word "Marine" would bring all kinds of powerful images to mind when anyone heard it.

Being a Marine had become synonymous with who I was. To me, being a Marine meant something powerful and good; therefore, I had those same values attached to me.

At the tender age of 18, I didn't leave home to join the circus — I became a Marine. When I joined the service, I realized I had been given a great gift — I was completely anonymous, and my drill instructors and could make my name mean whatever I proved it to be.

It just so happens I wanted my name to be associated with excellence, so I worked hard, earned three meritorious promotions, and after two years was offered the rank of Staff Sergeant, E-6. Achieving that rank was a rare occurrence for a 20-year-old Marine.

The home I left when I joined the service was good in many ways, but also turbulent in many more. My father was a recovering alcoholic who, in the years leading up to my departure, had been a difficult person to live with. His behavior brought our family a lot of instability. Also, he was not, I suspect, particularly fond of me, since I showed up unexpectedly when he was 45 years old.

Everything I knew about life and felt about myself up to that point had been learned in my home environment. I wasn't pleased with where I was and who I was, and I only wanted to get away. I feared my home life, with all its drama and stress, meant I would continue to live that way forever.

Not true.

The first thing I learned in Marine boot camp was that I wasn't tied to anyone or anything from my past — I was just me. The only thing I brought with me was my name: Dick Overton. If I wanted people to think highly of me, I could make that happen. All I had to do was earn their respect through my words and actions. I realized it was important to me what people thought when they heard my name. That was when I started to leave that troubled home life behind — it was my cornerstone.

When I left home, I was confused, angry, unhappy, and I had no idea who I was or where my life was going. That all changed quickly when I realized the opportunity the Marines afforded me. By the time I graduated from boot camp, I had earned one of my five meritorious promotions — Private First Class (PFC) — which was awarded among approximately sixty-plus recruits.

Before he left to take up his next platoon, one of my drill instructors took me aside and said something to me that, to this day, brings a lump to my throat. This man was a Marine's Marine. He was an infantry Marine with a tour in Vietnam under his belt, as well as a Purple Heart, among other awards. This was a guy we all respected. "Overton," he began, "I've watched you here, and I just want you to know if I was in a bad spot, I'd be glad to have you with me."

This was the first time I remember truly taking pride in my name and who I was becoming. I realized my name was mine and whatever people thought when they heard it was going to be determined by how I conducted myself from this point forward. It was all up to me.

This is the same concept Mike Siver is talking about in this book. The one thing we all carry with us as we navigate the world is our name, and we are responsible for the values that are attached to it.

After reading *Your Name,* I quickly recalled the number of times I had used the "your name" principle the book discusses throughout my career. Almost without realizing it, I had also often mentored work associates and young people by making them care about their names too. It's a simple idea, and one everyone can identify with — everyone has a name.

Convincing someone how valuable their name is, and just how much power they have to control the life attached to that name is a gift. Opening someone's eyes to this fact is one of the best things you can do for a person.

This book's powerful message speaks to any person, whatever their age, who is struggling to break away from their past and build a bright future. It talks about the one thing we all own, something that is ours to make of what we will — our name. The choice is truly yours — you can build your name into a shining example of everything good or you can let your name be associated with everything that's wrong in the world.

If you want to polish your name until it shines, you'll find the answers for how to start that journey within the pages of this book.

The time to begin is now.

Richard Overton

Preface

Our roles in life change over time, both through various choices we make and sometimes due to circumstances beyond our control. The way to take charge of your life and build a solid foundation for your name is to exert control over the choices you make, and pay attention to how you play the roles life hands you.

If you are trying to increase the value of your name, it is important to ask yourself: "Why did I do that?" when looking back on bad decisions or actions, and "What role do I play?" when thinking about your part in various situations in your life.

Author Mike Siver uses a practical, down-to-earth style to explain the oftentimes complex problems people encounter in their lives. He presents examples and provides real and simple to understand information to better equip you with the tools you will need to bring about a change in your life.

It is a pleasure to know Mike and the wonderful work he does for families and people in need. The book you're about to read will capture your attention and help you better understand why building respect for the name you are given is so important.

I remember asking Mike what made him chose the topics he writes about. His answer was, "If you can empower kids in destructive environments and show them how to learn about trust — you can work wonders in the world." Those words inspired me to continue my studies, and interestingly enough, I now work in Pediatrics, specializing in Indigenous Australian's health.

Mike also openly talks about his past problems and behaviors that led him on a destructive path early in his life, and then describes how he found a new path to success and service for others.

There is not much Mike hasn't done! He has been in the armed forces and worked on offshore oil rigs near Lebanon, plus I'm sure he's had some other adventures I haven't learned about yet.

His life experiences make it easy for him to relate to all sorts of people who are dealing with problems of all kinds. He uses non-judgmental compassion and his understanding of life to help people find their way in this world.

If you are ready to change your attitude and behavior and reinvent yourself so that your name is something to be proud of, Mike is your man! It is a pleasure to know him and the excellent work he does. He is a humble man who goes about doing God's Earthly Work.

Nita Sharp ND
Bachelor of Applied Science (Naturopath),
Masters in Nutrition Medicine
Ph.D. – Medicine / Indigenous Primary

Introduction

It takes many good deeds to build a good reputation,

and only one bad one to lose it.

— Benjamin Franklin

As you work your way through this book you will encounter examples of different situations, ways to positively change your name and examples of things you can do to reach your desired result. It is the author's hope that readers will learn that without integrity, understanding, and forethought, actions and behaviors can destroy your name or possible the name of someone close to you.

A "good name," i.e. integrity, is not something we are given — it must be earned. Because we aren't born with it, children rely on their parents and other influential adults in their lives to teach them to be honest and instill in them strong moral principles. Children receive this knowledge from adults more from observing actions than words. So, as parents and responsible adults, we need to be sure we are always acting as good role models.

Making your name synonymous with integrity, honesty, responsibility, and all the other good attributes we aspire to is not a one and done proposition. The purpose of this book is to show the reader how your name should be cared for and nurtured from birth to old age.

"What you do speaks so loudly that I cannot hear what you say."

— Ralph Waldo Emerson

Your Name and
Its Perceived Value
from Birth through Old Age

CHAPTER 1

Name-Building
Starts at Birth

Take personal responsibility in your daily endeavors and act as if every-

thing you do and say has your name on it...

Because it does!

The way others perceive you and what type of person they believe you to be becomes the reality they associate with you. It's up to you to be sure their perceptions are good ones based upon your actions, both past and present.

When you were born, your parents most likely put a lot of thought into choosing your name. This is one of the things they give to you that will be with you for the rest of your life. By choosing that special name for you, your parents were trying to give you a positive start in life.

Just as choosing your name was important to your parents, keeping that original positive association with it should be just as important to you throughout your life. If you don't respect your name, no one else will either!

If you doubt the mention of a name can color people's view of you, consider the immediate emotional response most people have to the names Jesus and Judas — one is extreme good and the other is the worst of the worst.

Jesus equals love and unselfishness. He was known for His honesty, integrity and for helping others and asking nothing in return. Judas, on the other hand, was known as a hypocrite, traitor and betrayer.

This example shows how much actions and how you treat people can influence other's perceptions of your name. When people only associate negative things with your name, it can significantly impact your life and future in a bad way.

"For you will certainly carry out God's purpose, however you act,

but it makes a difference to you whether you serve like

Judas or like John."

— C.S. Lewis, *The Problem of Pain*

NAME PERCEPTIONS START EARLY

It is important for parents to realize that our names can become tarnished, even at a young age. Consider these examples:

> If you baby-sit for the Smiths, get ready because their boy Charlie is a real handful. He is into everything, and his parents spoil him and he thinks he can do no wrong. He's got his mom and dad completely fooled and only acts up when they aren't around. They won't believe you when you tell them you should be paid extra because you had to put up with his extremely bad behavior.

> OR

> You're a lucky baby-sitter if you watch the Smith's boy, Charlie. He's a joy to be around and has such good manners. His parents are certainly doing something right with the way they're raising him.

The child and parents in both examples have things attached to their names in these two conversations. In the first example, the child's name is already earning the negative perceptions of bad behavior and manipulation, while his parents have the poor parenting and being fooled by their child perception attached to their names. In the second example, the child has good behavior and nice manners attached to his name, while his parents are perceived as caring and intelligent.

People often don't think about how their actions, even when they're quite young, can impact their lives for years to come. They also might think that any bad behavior which doesn't happen in public doesn't count because no one outside their immediate family knows about it. This type of thinking masks the problem, which will most likely start to spill over into other aspects of the child's life if not corrected quickly by parents or other influential adults.

In this case, a negative association with the child's name is probably already happening within the home too. If the child continuously misbehaves, parents or other adults might say things like, "Any time something is broken around here, there's a good chance Charlie broke it" or "Susie doesn't seem to care that she's in trouble all the time. She really is a problem child."

Once this perception is established, Susie and Charlie will have to work twice as hard to remove the negative association their names have already earned. If they're lucky, caring adults will step in and help them repair their names before the behaviors and associations are picked up outside their homes.

HARMFUL COMPARISONS

Another situation children might face when trying to build their names involves comparisons to siblings or other high-achieving classmates or teammates. A teacher, coach or parent might think that comparing a straight-A earning student or natural athlete sibling to one who is struggling is providing motivation for the struggling child to do better. Little do they know, they're actually causing the child to attach phrases like "not good enough" and "failure" to their name. To make matters worse, if this is done publicly it can cause other children to those associations too.

A study of twins by the Nuffield Foundation helps to prove that siblings, while having the same DNA, do not naturally have the same abilities. Thus, parents who expect their children to all have the same talents and academic achievements are setting themselves and their children up to fail.

Aimed at identifying specific environmental factors that influence achievement, well-being and decision-making during the educational transition at age 16, the Nuffield study's preliminary findings have shown that nurture (care and encouragement of growth) rather than nature (genetics) has the biggest influence on how children navigate the journey to adulthood. Even though the inherited DNA in twins is identical, the study points out that their different life outcomes have to be caused by differences in their experiences and their individual personalities.

Informal conclusions from this study indicate that setting a successful transition from primary school to secondary school, teacher-pupil relationships, socializing (both real and virtual) and bullying are all experiences that can exert influence on young people independent of their genes and have a major impact on the way they mature.

So, instead of comparing children to others, adults can foster a growth mindset by helping them develop problem-solving skills, set and meet goals, learn from their mistakes and face challenges with resilience rather than fear. It is important to realize that each child is an individual, and his or her achievements and/or difficulties should not be compared to those of others.

GENDER

Your gender can also have a big impact on the way people view your name. There is a definite double standard in our culture that says we expect girls to be better behaved and more in control than boys, even at an early age.

Ever heard the saying, "Boys will be boys," uttered as misbehaving male youngsters are forgiven their misdeeds? There is no similar saying or belief associated with girls. While it often happens subconsciously, parents, teachers and other authority figures can be guilty of perpetuating this double standard.

As children progress to the teenage years, this double standard shifts a bit. At this age, girls have to work to protect their names but boys are practically congratulated on their bad behaviors, especially by their peers. Therefore, young females must work harder to make sure their name isn't associated with bad behavior.

Many females, including my daughter, Haans Siver, do not think parents should raise their children with this gender discrimination-based double standard. Most feel that girls and boys should be treated with equal respect, equal boundaries/punishments, and be given equal opportunities to study and excel in their lives.

While this concept of gender equality may sound good, it's more difficult to put into practice for parents who want to protect their daughters from dangers most boys don't face. This means parents have to find a way to overcome the urge to be controlling and overprotective of their daughters so that they can offer them the same opportunities as their sons while still keeping them safe.

I believe most fathers remember quite clearly how they thought and acted when they were teen-aged boys, and it gives them nightmares and makes them want to lock their daughters in tall towers and not let them out until they're 30. I know this is how I felt when my daughter was growing up.

If I had it to do over again with my daughter, I would work much harder to explain why the double standard was in place in our household and I would also place my trust in her, rather than transferring my distrust of boys to her. Make no mistake, though, there would still be strict rules for dating and attending parties.

At the same time, I would also have conversations with my sons about why their sister didn't get to enjoy the same freedoms they had, and then explain why. I would also set a standard of behaviors and boundaries for dating and attending parties for them as well.

Looking back, I realize I allowed my sons to be the same kind of boys I was trying to keep my daughter away from. This was not my finest hour as a parent.

Despite my parental fumble with my daughter, she grew up to be a proud, mature, responsible woman who has a job where she's accountable for extremely expensive equipment and the staff that operates it.

This goes to show that parents never stop learning how to become better parents. As a parent you are your child's first teacher and should remain their best teacher throughout life.

"When you hold your baby in your arms the first time,
and you think of all the things you can say and do to influence him,
it's a tremendous responsibility.
What you do with him can influence not only him,
but everyone he meets and not for a day or a month or a year
but for time and eternity."

— Rose Kennedy

CHAPTER 2

Your Name as a Parent

Parents are the ultimate role models for children. Every word, movement and action has an effect. No other person or outside force has a greater influence on a child than the parent.

— Bob Keeshan

When you become a parent, you add a new name to the one you've already built for yourself — mother or father. The traits you've already been working to associate with your name will now become even more important because your children will be learning those same traits by association and example. These should include honesty, integrity, fairness, respect, caring and love.

As a parent, you are your child's role model. So, it's more important than ever to be aware of how you act and speak, because you're going to see your behavior parroted back to you by your child.

PARENTING STRATEGIES

While each child is an individual and every parent chooses how to parent their child, there are some constants that should be a part of every parent's arsenal.

Unconditional Love. First and most important of these is unconditional love. This comes naturally for many parents, but they can't just feel it, they also must demonstrate it to their children. Unconditional love is selfless and gives children a sense of security that will last throughout their lives.

Children who know that they are loved, no matter what, feel a great sense of security and tend to have more positive feelings about themselves. Unconditional love also allows children to feel okay about not being perfect, because they know their parent will forgive their mistakes and help them find the right path.

Here's where many people, including parents, lose their way in trying to give unconditional love. It is not ignoring issues that need corrected, making unnecessary sacrifices and trying to meet your loved one's needs at the expense of your own, or giving blanket tolerance to bad behavior. Children need boundaries and rules and a parent needs to be the one who cares enough to teach them right from wrong, not someone who allows them to run wild and misbehave while tolerating this behavior under the guise of unconditional love.

Affection. While all parents love their children, it's important to express that love to the child, both physically and through spending quality time with him or her to impart the message that they are valued and loved by you.

Communication. It's as important to listen to your child as it is to talk to them. Explaining your reasons for the rules you expect them to follow is a good place to start. Children tend to respond better when they know why a rule exists rather than just being told they must obey it. Reasoning with your child will also help them learn self-regulation so that they will obey the rules, even when no one is watching.

Responsibility. It is important for children to learn to accept responsibility for themselves and their actions. To do this, set limits, say no when needed, enforce established house rules, set expectations, assign chores around the house and follow through with consequences when rules are not followed.

Developing your child's sense of personal responsibility early and sticking with those lessons will help them succeed in school and later in the workplace and society at large. Responsible people's names are connected with doing what they say they're going to do.

Be positive. Emphasize what your child is doing well rather than what they're doing wrong. Pointing out good behaviors encourages your child to continue those behaviors. This will in turn make the child think more positively about themselves.

HOUSE RULES

Setting limits for children is a way to help them internalize good behavior. By setting house rules, you are giving your child a set of guidelines for good behavior as well as letting them know there are consequences for not following those rules.

The key to making this work so that your child learns responsibility is being consistent. It is vital that parents agree on the rules, how they will be enforced and the consequences for not following said rules. Presenting a united front, especially if the parents are no longer together, gives the child a stable environment and also stops them from playing one parent against the other to try to circumvent the rules.

Family House Rules. Parents need to set "family" house rules that apply to *everyone* in the family — yes, that means parents too — and then assign each individual child additional age-appropriate rules. Family house rules can be things like everyone takes their shoes off and puts them neatly by the door whenever they enter the house from outside, no climbing or jumping on furniture, no yelling inside the house, no interrupting when someone is speaking, always telling the truth, and saying please when asking for something and thank you when receiving something, and always saying you're sorry when you've done something wrong. These are simple rules that even the youngest in the family can understand and follow.

The consequences for not following these rules should also be explained, and then consistently applied any time the rules are broken. These consequences also apply to the parents if they break the rules.

Doing this will establish fairness and let children know that following the rules applies to everyone, not just them.

Example of consequences for family rules could be: sweeping the floor to remove the dirt that was tracked inside when shoes were worn inside the house, or apologizing to each family member individually when yelling happens inside the house. Consequences don't have to be huge, but they do need to be there to help teach children personal responsibility.

Individual House Rules. Separate rules for each child, tailored to age, are also a good idea. Below are some examples for kindergarten, grade school and teen individual rules.

A kindergarten-aged or younger child could have these rules: always ask permission to borrow other people's things, no hitting or kicking, and no name-calling. The consequences for breaking these rules could be things like a loss of privileges (a favorite toy being put away for a set amount of time) or a time-out for children who don't like to sit still. Again, the consequences for these infractions are small but will have a punitive meaning to the child, which will help them learn.

Grade school aged children can take on a bit more responsibility, probably an addition of 5-7 additional rules. These rules could be things like when you take something from its assigned place you must also put it back when you are finished with it, dirty clothes belong in the hamper, homework must be finished and checked by a parent before electronic games are played. Or they could be additional chores around the house like wiping bathroom and/or kitchen counters, feeding pets or clearing the table after meals.

Consequences for breaking these rules could be the child isn't allowed to use the item that wasn't put back for a set amount of time, the child will have to collect siblings' clothing and put it in the hamper for a set amount of time or electronic gadgets will be "outlawed" for a set amount of time. Again, nothing earth-shattering in the grand scheme of things, but they will matter to your child.

Teens can handle even more rules. These can be observing curfews, mandatory check-ins when out with friends, specific times and places where electronics are acceptable or taking on more chores like brining in the mail, taking out the trash, walking the dog, or loading and unloading the dishwasher.

Consequences for teens change slightly to reflect what is important to them. They can be things like losing electronic device use for a set time, being grounded (not allowed to socialize with friends outside of the home), or being given additional chores.

When children see there is a consistent pattern of consequences for breaking the rules, they will learn to make better choices. This will also help them as they mature, because these good behaviors will be attached to their names and adults and other children will view them favorably.

Something parents sometimes forget is that positive reinforcement is also important. So, when you notice your child is doing well following the "no yelling inside" rule, be sure to tell them what a good job they're doing. Praise can help motivate your child to continue following the rules, as well as give them a feeling of satisfaction and accomplishment.

Acknowledging them does not mean paying them or buying things for them. If you feel they deserve a reward above your praise, give them something intangible like letting them to stay up a little longer on a Friday night or allowing extra video game time. This type of thing should not be a given, it should only be earned with exceptional behavior. Giving rewards for doing things children are just enough to get by creates an attitude of entitlement, which is not something you want attached to your child's name.

WHY MAKE RULES?

Because we are social beings, we rely on interactions with others to thrive. To avoid chaos, we have created social norms we all agree on to dictate acceptable ways for us to behave. This helps our society function efficiently. Breaking these rules means facing predetermined consequences. By giving our children things like house rules and then adding individual rules to the list, we are helping to prepare them to function well in society.

Children may feel like they have too many rules, since they have to follow house rules, individual rules and rules at school. That makes it even more important that you explain why the rules are exist. You might start the conversation like this:

Imagine what life would be like with no rules. Anyone could take anything they wanted, including your stuff. People who don't know how to drive could jump in cars and drive wherever they wanted, including on the sidewalks and in people's yards. It wouldn't be safe to walk around anywhere because everything would be out of control and dangerous. What if everyone in your class could just talk whenever they wanted or get up and wander around while the teacher is talking? Do you think you'd learn anything that way?

Rules are created to bring order to the chaos that would exist otherwise. They can be used to keep people safe, enforce fairness, or teach responsibility and morals. In general, life runs more smoothly when we follow the rules, and those who break the rules face consequences.

As a parent, setting rules and enforcing them also makes the job of parenting easier. You want to raise children whose names include responsible and cooperative, and setting boundaries is essential for this to happen. Rules are not meant to quash the spirit, they're needed to help children flourish in society. The ways they do this include:

Preparation for the real world. Rules give children a framework for understanding what is expected and that there will be consequences for non-compliance.

Socialization skills are learned by practicing basic manners. Saying please and thank you at home will make your child pleasant to be around and give them the tools to function in polite society.

A sense of order is established when rules are set and followed. This allows the child to cooperate better when they know what's required of them.

Reassurance comes from children counting on their parents to guide their behavior. While children often think they want to be in control, having too much control is frightening and they need their parents' guidance.

Safety is achieved through rules, even if children often view these types of rules as taking the fun out of things. By insisting on following safety rules like wearing a helmet when bike riding, parents are preparing children to follow laws when they get older.

Rules can be confidence boosters if you gradually increase their limits as they mature. This helps to instill independence and an ability to handle responsibility in your child.

Ultimately, establishing and enforcing rules for your family is yet another way you can show them you love them. By setting boundaries early, you are helping to build a responsible and independent child who will have the confidence to achieve great things, and those are all things you want to be associated with your child's name.

> *"Parents, don't provoke your children in a way*
> *that ends up discouraging them."*
> — Colossians 3:21

CHAPTER 3

Building Your Name in Early Childhood

"It is easier to build strong children than to repair broken men."

— Frederick Douglass

As we discussed earlier, naming their child is the first thing parents do after their child is born. After that initial name choice, the true building of the child's name will come to represent begins. The early years are the most critical learning years of our lives, and oftentimes what we learn during this time continues to be a part of us for the rest of our lives.

Initially, children are influenced by parents, grandparents and a few select adults in their lives. But, when they reach the age where they start preschool, that insulated lifestyle changes drastically. Suddenly, children must interact with teachers, school aids, bus drivers, etc. as well as other children who can all possibly erode the good foundation you've been building for your child's name.

You might think that there isn't much need to worry about your child's name when they are this young. Unfortunately, even very young children can tarnish their names through bad behavior, whether learned from friends or reinforced by mimicking the behaviors of adults. While a few tantrums, arguments, and acts of defiance are acceptable, if such behaviors become daily occurrences, then there is cause for concern.

Some behaviors that could become problems include:

- Lying: to get attention, avoid getting into trouble or to feel better about themselves.
- Defiance: ignoring parents, saying no to requests, excessively testing limits.
- Disrespect: name-calling, mocking, throwing things to gain attention.
- Whining: to get what a child wants or to indicate disappointment.
- Lack of Impulse Control: hitting when displaying anger or blurting out unkind statements that hurt people's feelings.
- Aggression: throwing things or having a meltdown when things don't go their way.
- Temper Tantrums: stomping, screaming and throwing themselves on the floor in an effort to gain attention or get what they want.

These types of behaviors can color the perceptions of everyone from parents and grandparents to neighbors and baby-sitters. The impact from these perceptions can have an effect on your youngster's life in many ways.

For example, if Johnny's mother knows that Jeff is prone to whining and temper tantrums, she probably won't want her child to have a play date with him because she doesn't want her child to see these bad behaviors and potentially mimic them.

At this young age, Jeff's name is already tarnished, and it's his parents' job to make sure they address these problems and redirect his behaviors before they are so ingrained that it will be difficult for him to change. His parents must also examine how they are dealing with these bad behaviors to make sure they aren't reinforcing them.

Here's an example of how parents can unwittingly encourage bad behavior:

A family with three young children has been going through some hard times recently. The parents are on edge and don't react well to discord from their children. As a result, their youngest child throws a tantrum whenever he wants to get his way, so the parents immediately give him what he wants so he will be quiet. By doing this, they have taught him that all he has to do is behave badly and he will get what he wants. The child is smart, figures this out quickly and uses this knowledge often.

Fixing this behavior means that rather than giving in each time their child throws a tantrum, the parents in should ignore the behavior so that the child gets the message that tantrums do not earn rewards. The parents should also show the child less manipulative and destructive ways to express his wants and needs so that he isn't causing them (and others) to associate his name with this manipulative behavior.

FRIENDS AND YOUR CHILD'S NAME

We are social animals, and as such have an inherent need to be liked and have friends in our lives, even from an early age. Before starting preschool, children's friends are generally based upon proximity, such as neighborhood children, relatives' children, and children of their parents' friends.

These influences are relatively easy for parents to control, since children are only really interested in having fun at this age and don't think much about what other children think of them or worry about how many friends they have.

As a result, these friendships are relatively transitory, i.e. "friends" are whoever the child happens to be paying with at the time. This also means parents don't have to worry too much about how these "friends" will influence their child's behavior.

As children enter preschool, forming friendships becomes more important because they help children develop life skills like getting along with other people, and start giving them the tools to start problem-solving. Children with these skills are less likely to have social and emotional difficulties later in life.

Play is a big part of how children connect with others and make new friends as they get older. If children are equipped with the skills needed to interact with others, there is a better chance that they will continue to choose friends who have similar interests and fit in well with the foundation you, as parents, have been building for your child's name.

Here are some things parents can teach their children to help ensure they make friends more easily:

- **Sharing:** For example, you might show your child a treat of some kind and say, "Let's share this treat — some for you and some for me."

- **Taking Turns:** When paying games, or merely kicking a ball, show the concept to your child by first kicking the ball yourself and saying, "My turn," then retrieve the ball and give it to your child and say, "Your turn." Also, when your child takes turns or shares something without being prompted, be sure to hand out liberal praise to help encourage them to continue this behavior. For example, "Good job sharing" or "Isn't it fun when we take turns?"

- **Respect:** Treat your child with respect so that they will do the same when dealing with others. While this might not seem relevant to making friends, teaching this concept by practicing it helps your child know how to treat others.

- **Communication:** Practice good communication skills and active listening at home to help teach your child how to communicate with others. Everyone likes to feel that people are paying attention when they talk, so modeling this for your child will help them to do the same when they interact with friends and potential friends.

- **Compromise:** Teach kids how to compromise so that they are able to resolve conflicts in a peaceful way. Kids who have siblings generally pick up this skill organically as they interact with their brothers and sisters. If your child butts heads with a friend, consider it a learning opportunity and help them come to a solution that will be acceptable to both sides.

- **Forgiveness:** Understanding and forgiveness are both important concepts to teach your child so that when needed, they won't be vindictive if they feel they've been wronged by someone. Encourage them to consider what happened from a different perspective. Was it an accident, was the other person just having a bad day, etc. Doing this will likely help kids give the transgressor the benefit of the doubt, thus defusing their anger.

[9]Two are better than one because they have a good return for their work, [10]If one falls down his friend can help him up. But pity the man who falls and has no one to help him up.
— Ecclesiastes 4: 9-10

MIMICKING GOOD BEHAVIOR

Young children are some of the most honest people in the world. They also remember and repeat pretty much everything they hear and see as they observe adults and older children they respect. Children remember the situation in which they saw or heard something and will repeat or use the same words and actions when they find themselves in a situation they feel is similar.

Problems can arise when what they saw and heard weren't really the best solutions for the situation and the child ends up being "in trouble" for the mimicked behavior. This creates a lot of confusion for the child.

As parents, we have to be continuously aware that we are being watched and listened to by our children and they are using what they see and hear as examples of how to behave. Therefore, we need to be careful about how our words and actions are perceived.

One of the ways to do this is to follow the same house rules you have set for your children. Some examples of these rules could be:

1. Always knock on closed doors before opening them. This teaches children about respecting personal space and common courtesy. Extending this same courtesy to them will help to reinforce the concept.

2. Shouting is not the way to make a point, calm and rational discussion is. Parents should be sure that they observe this rule, especially when dealing with disciplining their children.

3. Being rude is not tolerated. For example, everyone in the household should say please when making a request, and thank you to show gratitude for the things others do for you. Everyone should also be kind, polite, courteous and respectful of others.

Parents who "practice what they preach" will find that their children are more inclined to follow the rules. Teaching children to follow rules also helps to create order and structure in the family and prepares children for the world outside the family. Most importantly, you're teaching your children how to value themselves and become a functioning part of society.

TEACHING LIFE SKILLS

Learning life skills can help your child protect their name by providing a map for how to live their lives successfully.

Just like a carpenter's toolbox, their life skills toolbox should be filled with what is needed to get the job done. The job, in this case, is finding your way in life.

Because many of the items we need in our toolbox are not things we were born with, parents must work to give their children these tools so that they can successfully build their good names as they grow up.

For example, a master carpenter would not hand his apprentice an expensive piece of hardwood and tell him to create an ornate shelf from it. He would first make sure the apprentice had the required skills and knew what was needed to complete the job, and he would do this by communicating using his years of experience, and then showing the apprentice with his actions.

Parents should help children learn in the same way. By showing their children good examples, as well as communicating important life lessons openly, parents can help children to become good people who make wise life choices. No matter what task we encounter as parents, how well or how poorly we deal with that task is the lesson we are showing our children.

For example, if we want them to have good personal and working relationships, then we will need to look at the role we play in teaching them these skills every day in real-life situations. Learning by example is the easiest way for children to understand. Therefore, as parents, we need to be very aware of the examples we are showing our children. Here are some simple examples of tools you should want your child to include in their toolbox:

- **Respectfulness: Observing the Golden Rule,** *"Do unto others as you would have them do unto you."* Set a good example for your children by showing them how to respect and be kind to others. When children see considerate behavior and watch you deal with good and bad situations in a respectful way, they learn how to behave the same way in their interactions.

- **Generosity: Helping others.** Whether you choose to volunteer your time as a family or donate resources such as clothes or canned food, it is important for your child to see you being generous so that he or she can learn the value of helping others.

- **Honesty and Integrity: Telling the truth in all situations and having strong moral principles.** Showing honesty by doing things like admitting you were wrong, speaking up when you see something wrong, and choosing not to cheat, as well as keeping promises, doing the right thing without expecting a reward and not gossiping when someone has told you something in confidence, are all good examples to set for your children. Seeing you behaving this way will mean they'll be more likely to model your behavior because those things engender trust.

- **Listen without prejudice:** Genuinely listen to what other people have to say, whether or not you agree with their comments, because that's one way we keep growing. Your child will notice your consideration for other people's thoughts and points of view, and will better learn how to think for him or herself.

- **Be Polite:** Always be polite to others, no matter the circumstances, whether in public or at home. This could be demonstrated by giving up your seat to an elderly person on a bus, holding a door open for a stranger, or simply saying "thank you." Setting this good example for your child will help them throughout life, because everyone appreciates politeness.

- **Consistency:** Aim to maintain consistent behavior in all aspects of your life by always behaving the same way in similar situations. You should not be polite to one person and turn around and be rude to someone else, or listen to some people and disregard others. Children thrive on consistency and stability, so when they see permanent, healthy parental consistency, they learn to emulate this behavior.

Other tools to include in your child's toolbox could be things like decision-making, starting with basics like choosing clothes for the day; health and hygiene, including things like taking a bath, brushing teeth, washing hands; and basic chores like putting toys away or wiping the toothpaste off the sink after they've brushed their teeth. While these things may seem small, they accumulate and help to attach responsibility, accountability, and integrity to your child's name. If these tools are used often, the good properties you're trying to teach will become second nature for your child.

"If the only tool you have in your toolbox is a hammer, everything and everyone you deal with will look like a nail."
— Abraham Maslow

CONCLUSION

While it may seem like worrying about how your child's name is perceived at this early age is a waste of time, it truly is not. This is the time that you, as a parent, help your children to start building their identity — and you want that identity to be a good one. So, teach your young children to be confident and define their names in authentic ways through their good choices, good behavior and good manners. Doing this will help to give them the armor they need to resist peer pressure and the stresses they will encounter as they grow up.

"Your destiny is not predetermined, It is determined by the choices you make and those you choose not to make."

—Deon Potgieter

"By wisdom a house is built, and by understanding it is established; by knowledge the rooms are filled with all precious and pleasant riches."

— Proverbs 24:3-4

CHAPTER 4

Building Your Name
Preschool–Grade School

"Children learn more from what you are than what you teach."

— W.E.B. Dubois

As children get a little older and are grouped together at school, they consciously start to think about how many friends they have and why some children might not want to be their friends. At this point, they realize that friendship goes beyond just playing together for the moment and they start to think in more pragmatic terms, such as defining friends as those who do nice things for them, like sharing treats, saving seats at lunch, etc. However, at this age they do not yet think about what they bring to the friendship.

During this stage of development, your child will start to view having friends as very important. He or she might even decide to put up with a not-so-nice child, just to add them to their friendship count. This is something parents should monitor, since this not-so-nice child could easily become a negative influence on your child's behavior and possibly start to erode all the work you've been doing to help build your child's name.

When parents notice this behavior, it is a great teaching moment. Addressing it will help your child as they navigate the changing landscape of friend-making throughout their school years. Explain how important it is to be your authentic self and be honest with friends. Suggest finding friends with similar interests. Also, talk to your child about how friends should treat one another, and what healthy and unhealthy exchanges look like.

UNDERSTANDING YOUR CHILD'S BEHAVIOR ISSUES

Unfortunately, undesirable labels can become attached to your child's name easily if the child has behavior problems in the classroom. As parents, we know how hard it is to get rid of those labels once they've been applied, and how devastating that association can be for a child.

Some behaviors have legitimate medical or psychological roots, and can be controlled with medication. So, it's important to consult professionals if you believe your child is experiencing these types of issues.

This is not to suggest that all problem behaviors need to be treated medically. A "magic pill" is not the way to make up for lack of parenting, nor is it a ready-made excuse for the child to use to explain their bad behavior. Your child should not be throwing around phrases like, "Oh, I know I shouldn't have done that, but I have ADHD, so it is not my fault."

As a parent, you are responsible for teaching your child life skills, responsibility, and that actions have consequences. This responsibility is ongoing and the lessons need to be reinforced daily. Unfortunately, when you are dealing with behavior issues, discipline will become necessary.

DISCIPLINE

There are five types of discipline you can use with your children. It's wise to tailor the discipline to fit both your parenting style and your child's personality.

1. POSITIVE DISCIPLINE

This type of discipline is based up on praise and encouragement, instead of punishment. With this method, parents should help their child identify the problem and develop multiple solutions to it, identifying the pros and cons of each. Then, ask the child which discipline he or she thinks will work. Once the child chooses a solution, they should then test it out to see what happens. If it doesn't work, then they need to try another solution.

This type of discipline takes the child's feelings into consideration, and allows them to be involved in solving the problem. This also encourages respectful communication between child and parent. When the problem is solved, the parents should encourage the child to continue to deal with problems in this way.

Here's an example: Your child refuses to do homework. Rather than just telling the child, "You have to do your homework or you cannot play baseball after school this week." Instead, ask your child why he/she doesn't want to do homework. The answer might surprise you. You might find out, for example, they don't understand the assignment and didn't want to admit their ignorance. In this case, you need to step in and help. Communication, rather than assumption, is key in all situations.

WHY USE POSITIVE DISCIPLINE?

- It teaches responsibility, self-discipline, problem-solving skills and cooperation.

- It is respectful to both children and adults.

- It builds trust and strengthens relationships, building new connections in the child's brain.

- It builds and maintains self-esteem.

- It teaches children how to manage their emotions.

- It teaches children to deal with stress in healthy ways.

- It invites children to contribute in meaningful ways.

- It develops strong understanding that one has power or influence over what happens to them in life.

2. GENTLE DISCIPLINE

Gentle discipline focuses on preventing problems and using redirection to steer children away from bad behavior. It acknowledges the child's feelings and spells out expectations. With this form of discipline, children are given negative consequences for their behavior, but are not shamed or embarrassed.

These consequences need to be effective and consistent, and they need to actually deter your child's behavior. For example, taking away TV privileges isn't effective if your child prefers to play games on his tablet. The consequences need to be specific to the child.

Some examples of negative consequences are:

Logical: These are directly related to the misbehavior. For example, if your child continues to leave his/her bike in the yard after you have asked them to put it away each evening, then the consequence would be they lose bike privileges for a week.

Ignoring: If your child constantly exhibits behavior like throwing a tantrum to get your attention, then ignoring the child might be the best negative consequence.

Time-out: If your child is active and doesn't like sitting still, using a time-out that requires them to sit quietly for a period of time might be a good way to encourage them to not repeat the bad behavior.

Added responsibility: If your child doesn't complete tasks you have asked him/her to do, adding extra chores as a consequence might be effective. For example, if your child didn't pick up his/her toys when they were done playing, the consequence could be to pick up the toys and then clean his/her room.

When implementing consequences, it is important for parents to be calm and consistent, especially when using negative consequences. Explain the reason the consequences came to be and talk about your child's behavior and how they can modify it in the future to avoid more negative consequences. The goal is to show kids how to better deal with the situation if they are faced with it again.

3. BOUNDARY-BASED DISCIPLINE

This form of discipline focuses on setting limits and making the rules clear from the beginning. Kids are given choices and told that there are clear consequences for misbehaving.

Setting limits as a parent gives children a guideline for behavior, but setting these limits can be difficult. For example, parents might feel guilty about saying no to something their child wants. If you're feeling guilty, just remember that limits are good for children and help to teach them appropriate behavior and self-discipline.

Children will test these boundaries, and parents need to stand firm. Consistency with enforcing house rules is extremely important. Once children realize there are limits and consequences for ignoring those limits, behavior problems will be reduced.

If you choose this method of discipline, here are some techniques that will be helpful:

- **Communicate Limits:** Establish clear house rules and even go so far as to print out the list and hang it on the refrigerator. If a situation arises where a house rule doesn't exist, be sure to set clear limits when dealing with your child.

- **Give warnings before enacting discipline:** If your child is dragging his or her feet about completing a task, etc. give a five-minute warning before discipline is employed. For example, you could say: "You have five minutes to finish playing your game and put it away. If you don't do that, you will not be allowed to go to your friend's house later."

- **Offer choices:** Outline choices to point out the results their behavior will have. You could say, "Stop what you're doing and set the table or keep doing what you're doing and lose your gaming privileges tomorrow." This allows your child to make the choice and take responsibility for his or her actions.

- **Logical consequences:** A logical consequence is directly related to the behavior. For example, taking away your child's tablet because he/she refused to turn it off when asked.

- **Natural consequences:** These type of consequences are great teaching tools that allow children to both learn from their mistakes and learn responsibility. If your child forgot to pack his/her soccer uniform, he/she will not be allowed to play in the game. While this might be upsetting to the child, the lesson will stay with them and they will make an effort to remember their uniform in the future.

Again, consistency is the key — don't bend the rules after you've set them. Each time a rule is violated, follow through with consequences, not nagging, lectures or anger. By doing this, you'll be helping your child learn right from wrong, accountability, decision-making skills and you'll be building a better relationship because following through shows you care.

4. BEHAVIOR MODIFICATION.

Behavior modification focuses on positive and negative consequences. Good behavior is praised or rewarded and misbehaving is discouraged with consequences like loss of privileges, etc.

Positive punishment involves adding a consequence that will deter your child from repeating the behavior in question. For example, giving your child an extra chore when they didn't complete one of their weekly chores.

Negative punishment is taking something away. This could be ignoring a temper tantrum (taking away your attention) or taking away video game privileges.

Positive reinforcement is giving your child something that reinforces good behavior. This can be as simple as saying "good job" when your child does something before you've asked them to do it.

Negative reinforcement is used to motivate your child to change their behavior because it will remove something they find unpleasant. An example would be your child is getting in trouble while waiting at the bus stop, so you start going with them to wait for the bus every day. The child is embarrassed to have his/her parent there and starts behaving better so that the parent will no longer come with to the bus stop. This type of reinforcement should be used sparingly so that it doesn't lose its effectiveness.

In the end, you cannot force your child to change his or her behavior, but you can motivate them to change for the better. As a parent, you can use behavior modification to create an atmosphere where your child has more incentive to follow the rules, as long as those rules are enforced consistently. You should also be sure to be a good role model for your children by following the rules as an adult, even going so far as to explain why a rule is good and should be followed even when breaking it is tempting.

By giving your child the tools to make good judgments you're helping them to be responsible, develop strong character, know right from wrong, and think for themselves. This will help to your child take charge of their life and make sure their name will always be polished to a high shine.

A PERSONAL NOTE:

I repeated the fourth grade, and it devastated me. In my mind, I was a failure. That one event affected me for a number of years. What made it worse in my young mind was I was now in the same grade as my younger sister. And worse yet, for the rest of my school years, I was continuously compared to my smart, attentive and well-behaved little sister.

For some reason, I thought that being popular would compensate for my poor grades. So, I worked very hard to be the best at track and got a varsity letter when I was in ninth grade. Then, I decided to go out for cheerleader. After a lot of practice, I tried out in front of the whole school and got selected for the squad. I felt good about being chosen, even though I suspected I was chosen because I was the only boy who tried out. I then joined the school choir, and was accepted, not because I was any good (I'm terrible), but because there were no other boys in the choir.

Even with all these activities and perceived popularity, my grades still weren't good. So, by the time I reached tenth grade, I'd had enough of the constant comparisons to my sister and I quit school. While quitting was my choice, the constant comparison and my feelings of being a failure were major contributors to my decision. When I think about it, I don't think I ever saw myself as a high school graduate — I set myself up to fail academically because I just gave up.

The constant comparisons to my sister were damaging to me too. I'm sure this was intended as motivation, but I saw it as negative and devaluing, and let it destroy my self-esteem.

Luckily for me, at that time you could enlist in the military without a high school diploma or GED. So, I did.

It took me many years to get over the stigma of my perceived academic failure. Years later, I finally found the courage to go back to school, and I loved it. When viewing education through mature eyes, I realized I wasn't competing with other students — I was being graded solely on my abilities.

I mistakenly attached "failure" to my name for years, and it effected my life in many negative ways. Could I have avoided this? Probably. I don't believe I ever explained to my parents or teachers how I felt or the problems I was having with learning. For me, those lines of communication just didn't feel open.

So, the moral of this story is, be careful what you say to children and with the comparisons you make to others in reference to their difficulties. Stop and truly think about what you're saying so that you don't inadvertently attach something negative to a child's name when all you want to do is be motivational and encouraging.

"Your children vividly remember every unkind thing you ever did to them, plus a few you really didn't.

— Mignon McLaughlin

CHAPTER 5

Building Your Name Middle School–High School

Keeping that communication channel open with your teen is one of the most important things as a parent you can do.

— C Pulsifer

Most adults know the pre-teen through teen years are the hardest and possibly the most challenging in our lives. Young people moving from childhood to becoming a teenager want to be treated like adults, even though they are still children. This can cause a lot of turbulence between parents and child.

This is also the time when children become consumed having lots of friends and being "popular." They will also sometimes start behaving differently in order to emulate their popular peers. The message children get about who they are and how the world works at this age will have an impact on their lives far into the future.

The quest for popularity is often rooted in uncertainty and insecurity about their bodies, how they fit into the family unit and who they are and what they want to be. They use groups of friends who are experiencing the same things to help them to feel normal. Because of this, their self-worth ends up being tied to the approval and acceptance of their peers.

The more certain they are of their peers' approval, the greater their sense of self will be. Thus, the quest for popularity, i.e. having lots of friends, becomes hugely important. Should parents disapprove of these new peers, things will become rocky.

UNDERSTANDING WITH POPULARITY

There are two types of popularity. The first is likability, which is the first form of popularity children experience. Children as young as three will be able to tell you the child they like the most at daycare. At this age, the children who are liked the most are the popular kids. Most likely these are the children who know how to share and make others feel good about themselves.

The second type of popularity is status. This type of popularity doesn't measure how well someone is liked by others, rather it reflects that person's visibility, dominance and influence on his or her peers. This is the type of popularity that first rears its ugly head during the middle school years, when our brains start to change and a neurochemical cocktail of oxytocin and dopamine promotes an urgent need to connect and bond with others. This status-seeking behavior is more like primate chest-beating than likability.

As parents, there's no real way to control the storm of hormones raging through your pre-teen/teen's body. Take heart though, because this is where the good foundation you built for your child's name during their early years acts as scaffolding that will provide a model of positive social behavior and help them navigate this turbulent time in their lives.

Now would also be a good time to reinforce the importance of the value of your child's name. Remind your child about the things you've been teaching them, including:

- Your name equals the public's impression of you based on your conduct and becomes how you are known socially.

- Your name is like your shadow self — it follows you through life, and the effect it has, good or bad, is dictated by your behaviors.

- Your name is going to be partly judged by your social associations and the peer groups you belong to — so choose friends wisely.

- How you act is how you are seen by others.

- The way people view your name (reputation) now can impact how you are treated in the future.

- It's hard to earn a good name, but even harder to live down a bad one.

- It works in your favor to always be on your best behavior.

- The crowd you hang out with can have a real-life impact on how others view your name.

Be sure to emphasize the fact that the value they are building for their name right now will travel with them into adulthood.

> *31Heaven and earth will pass away,*
>
> *but My words will by no means pass away.*
>
> — Mark 13:31-37

PROBLEM FRIENDSHIPS

Parents should pay close attention to what their children say when they talk about what goes on at school, as well as the what they're saying about the things their friends have done and said. This is a great way to know when to redirect any undesirable behavior before it becomes a problem.

If your child mentions something that troubles you, act quickly to address the situation in a calm and caring manner. This is not the time to get angry with your child or make threats like, "Stay away from Billy, he's a bad influence on you!" Reactions like this almost always get the opposite of the desired effect.

If you're asking your child to make changes in their friendships, you should explain the reasons for your request rather than just ordering them to change. Remember, their self-worth is tied to their friendships. They value their friends and will not want to end a friendship without a valid reason.

Explaining why will help smooth the way. Saying something like, "Your friend doesn't take school seriously and is constantly getting into trouble. I know you like him/her, but I don't want you to start acting like that too. You're a good student and you respect your teachers. I just don't want you to think that the way your friend acts is the way you should act."

After saying this, engage your child in a discussion about the friend's behavior and ask them how they feel about it and what they think their association with that friend is doing to their name.

If your child is the one saying or doing things that are troublesome, your swift and caring action is also needed here. Parents don't want their child to be branded as a "troublemaker," since that can end up destroying the child's self-esteem/self-image. Plus, if they are labeled that way often enough, they can start to believe that is who they are and act accordingly.

So, rather than telling your child they are "bad" or "worthless" or any number of other negative things, instead reinforce their positive behaviors by praising them so the child, who craves parental approval, will choose those behaviors more often.

As parents, it's also good to help your child model healthy relationships. You can do this with personal stories, books, and movies that spotlight important qualities—both positive and negative—in friends.

Children this age are capable of having deep, rewarding friendships, yet they are still learning the rules of social interaction and communication. Some children seem to learn these rules intuitively, while others can benefit from direct teaching, so parents need to stay involved. Make sure your child knows that your input, guidance and support will be there to help them every step of the way, without being intrusive. The experiences your child has during this time are paving the way for satisfying friendships in the future.

Whatever emotional state you're in while parenting conveys more to your child than the content of what you're doing with them, no matter how perfect your intervention looks "on paper." In other words, to paraphrase Marshall McLuhan, "your emotional state is the message."

— Michael Y. Simon, *The Approximate Parent: Discovering the Strategies that Work for Your Teenager*

GOSSIP AND LIES

Being the subject of untrue, hurtful gossip can feel like the end of the world for your teen. They experience a sense of powerlessness and a need for revenge that can backfire. It's your job, as a parent, to prevent your teen from "giving as good as they got" by retaliating in kind. At its core, this type of gossip is bullying, and you do need to deal with it, but you need to do it without causing more damage.

Make sure your teen knows you support them by listening to them vent about the experience. They need to know that even though things at school are bad for them right now, you still have their back.

Once your teen has calmed down a bit, discuss how to handle damage control. Counsel them to refute the rumor/gossip once, and then be done with it so that it doesn't have more power over them than it should. Let them know that they just have to let it go, no matter how difficult it seems.

If the gossip was posted on social media, check the site's terms. If the post violates them, report the post and urge that it be taken down. Then advise your teen to refute the post once, then not to engage after that. Internet trolls live for drama, and you don't want to feed the trolls. Let the post lose momentum.

While finding the silver lining in this situation can be difficult, it is a good time to teach your teen about the value of true friendship. True friends will stick by you no matter what and will support you fully.

You can also encourage your teen to practice resiliency by helping them understand what is important and what isn't. In other words, the opinion of the mob doesn't matter, knowing yourself and having the support of friends and family does.

If the gossip/bullying behavior persists, it's probably time for you, as a parent, to step in and involve the relevant parties, including school officials and the gossip's parents. While few cases of gossip, rumor or even bullying require intervention by the authorities, if the matter is serious enough, it should be reported to the police. Every state has either anti-bullying policies or laws to protect victims of bullying.

GUILTY BY ACCUSATION

*How many times have rumors caused you to form
a negative opinion of someone?*

*How many times have untrue rumors been spread
about you or your family?*

*Reputations, families, and lives can be destroyed
just because of false accusations.*

*If you want to hurt someone,
all you have to do is make an accusation.*

Accusations are one of the most powerful weapons used today.

Gossip, Rumors, and False Accusations all mean the same thing — spreading false information about another person.

One would think we get we would grow out of this behavior, but adults are sometimes more calculating and vicious. We all need to remember the destructive power of unproven accusations and avoid making them at all costs, because they can have a devastating effect on your name and the names of others that can be next to impossible to repair.

*Puberty is such a confusing time. You are still a child, with all that
wonderful naivete and innocence, but your body is changing, and you're
self-conscious and curious about its impact on others all at the same time.*

— Maimouna Doucoure

PUBERTY STRIKES AND YOUR CHILD CHANGES

The hormones that transform children to young adults will seriously disrupt your child's emotions. They can be acting like a child one minute and the next minute seem like an adult — and they want to be treated like an adult all the time, regardless of how they're acting.

What's worse for them is their body seems to be turning on them in the form of fluctuating energy levels, mood swings, acne, oily hair, body odor, hair sprouting where it didn't grow before and extreme sensitivity to any mention of said changes.

These tips may be useful when dealing with your moody teen:

- Praise your teen for their efforts, achievements and positive behavior.

- Realize your child is struggling to become an individual and understand when they try to push boundaries.

- Stay calm during angry outbursts and wait for the child to calm down before talking about the problem. Understand that they're trying to learn to regulate their emotions while dealing with hormone storms.

- Stay interested and involved in your child's life and make sure they know you're always available to talk.

- Support your child's self-expression, even if it seems odd. This could include an extreme haircut, brightly colored hair, different clothing choices, etc.

- Talk to your child about permanent changes they want to make to their body and strongly suggest temporary alternatives.

BODY IMAGE

Maintaining a healthy, normal body image during puberty, a time of major physical and emotional changes, can be difficult. This is a time when teens compare their bodies to those of their friends and worry about how their development compares. Below are a few things you can do to help them realize these are normal changes everyone experiences:

Set a good example. As a parent, you should listen to your child's concerns in a non-judgmental way, show them you understand where they're coming from and explain that bodies develop on their own schedule and come in all shapes and sizes. You should also set a good example for your teen by showing them how you accept your body as it is and talk to them about the fact that there is no "perfect" body.

Use positive language. Instead of talking about physical attributes, praise his or her personal characteristics like strength of character, persistence and kindness. Avoid pointing out negative physical attributes in others or yourself, and certainly don't use hurtful nicknames or jokes based upon a person's physical characteristics.

Explain puberty. List all of the possible changes a body goes through during puberty so that your child knows that all of the strange things he or she is experiencing are normal.

Media messages. Talk about all of the conflicting messages they will encounter on social media, in movies and television, and in magazines. Make sure they understand that much of what they see from these sources has been altered and doesn't exist in real life, so they are not looks to aspire to.

INDEPENDENCE

It's normal for your teen to want more independence at this time, but still need a lot of support from you. This push for independence may worry you, but try to stay calm and work through each issue that comes up. Communicate openly and make sure your child knows you're available to listen any time they need you.

Reinforce the good decision-making skills you've already instilled in your child, and show them you trust them by giving them slightly more independence. This could be something like a later curfew, with the stipulation that they tell you where they're going and what they're doing, or driving themselves to school. Also let them know the consequences for breaking the rules associated with these more independent actions.

Your teen is also going to be working hard to establish his or her unique name (identity). This could mean new friendships and new experiences that help expand their understanding of their social world. They may also start to explore their sexual identity through romantic relationships and dating. These explorations can help to create a foundation of how to engage in healthy relationships as well as how to identify unhealthy relationships, so be sure you're available for questions when needed.

FEMALE-SPECIFIC ADVICE

While puberty occurs in both males and females, each gender has certain changes specific to it. These changes are both physical and psychological, and can cause confusion, fear and even anger. It's important that parents explain these changes so that the child knows what to expect and realizes this is a normal part of growing up.

Physical changes can include widening hips, breast growth and tenderness, hair growth, periods and the pain associated with them, acne and body odor.

Emotional changes can include mood swings and changes in sleep patterns and requirements due to hormone changes, feeling self-conscious about physical changes (or lack thereof), sexual interest, and feelings of frustration with house rules due to a greater sense of self and a need for more independence.

This is a difficult time for both the child and the parents. Erratic behaviors and acting out can cause frustration and quick, intense emotional changes can make for a turbulent home life for everyone involved. The adults in the situation need to remember their own journey through puberty and be patient and understanding as their child rides this hormonal roller coaster.

MALE-SPECIFIC ADVICE

While some of the changes boys experience during puberty are the same as girls, including acne, hair growth, height and muscle growth, and body odor, there are others that are specific to the male of our species, several of which are sexual in nature.

Because puberty can take place between ages nine and 14 in boys, many of the late bloomers have problems watching their peers develop before they do. Parents can help their child make it through this time by not commenting on the child's friend's growth spurt, deeper voice, etc. and avoid teasing about anything puberty/development related. Instead, reassure your child that he will eventually catch up.

Children who experience earlier puberty can have just as much anxiety as those who develop later. Parents can help ease this anxiety by treating the changes as normal and by introducing the child to rituals of approaching manhood like shaving, applying deodorant/antiperspirant, etc.

Pubescent boys experience voice changes, genital growth, wet dreams and erections. While the "funny sounding" voice changes are relatively harmless and easy for most boys to deal with, those changes related to sex organs aren't.

Some boys will have worries about penis size and compare theirs to other boys of their age. They will also be embarrassed by uncontrollable erections that happen for what seems like no reason at all, and the occurrence of wet dreams (ejaculation during sleep). All of these things can cause feelings ranging from embarrassment to shame and be difficult for your child to talk about.

In this case, parents should discuss that both nocturnal emissions (wet dreams) and erections are a natural occurrence at this age and are the body's response to a sudden increase in testosterone levels. Sudden and frequent sexual thoughts and desires, along with frequent erections are also normal. Avoid showing disapproval or teasing about these experiences. Instead, make sure to educate your son about what they mean and let him know that you are always available for questions or advice.

CHANGES TRUE FOR BOTH

Acts of rebellion and impulsively saying or doing things out of character are to be expected from both boys and girls. The parents' job at this point is to make sure that the emerging sex drive and raging hormones their child is dealing with don't take them down a road that will ruin all of the hard work they've put into building their name up to this point.

Many young people going through puberty are confused about their place in the grand scheme of things. Compounding this confusion is the fact that they are starting to have the outward appearance of adulthood but their brains and emotions are playing catch up. As parents, you will need to recognize this confusion and help your child navigate through it.

Good, calm communication is key, as well as making sure your child knows they can come to you with questions and concerns. Children this age often worry that the adults in their lives won't take them seriously, or that they will somehow be in trouble if they tell you their problems.

Engender trust by helping your child sort through the problem so that you can both see the situation clearly. Then, identify options or solutions to the problem so that your child knows he or she is not alone and there is someone who cares and shares the same feelings. Also encourage your child to never keep problems to themselves. Doing so causes tension that can lead to emotional outbursts and acting out.

INCREASED INDEPENDENCE

This time in your child's life is a battle between his or her adolescence and emerging adulthood. What this means is you, as a parent, are going to have to start giving your child some more independence. This doesn't mean treating them as a full-fledged adult, but it does mean loosening your grip a little. This could be something like allowing your teen to drive him or herself to school, giving them more privacy at home, or implementing a slightly later curfew.

While giving these small independence-related things, this is also the time to clarify your house rules and make clear that these new "gifts" will be taken back should the rules not be followed. Don't be afraid to be disliked by your child when you enforce the rules — as a parent it is not your job to be liked, it's your job to keep your child safe and ensure they grow up to be responsible, caring adults.

No matter when you were born or where, puberty is the same. It's the same for your parents as it is for you - what's happening in your body dictates everything.

— Francine Pascal, author of young adult books

CHAPTER 6

Building Your Name in Young Adulthood

High school is what kind of grows you into the person you are. I have great memories, good and bad, some learning experiences and some that I'll take with me the rest of my life.

— Giancarlo Stanton

By the time young people reach this age, they may feel that the topic of character development is "uncool." But, as parents, it's up to you to make them understand that it's anything but uncool. There's nothing uncool about success, and that's what having good character associated with your name will achieve for you.

Most parents have been helping their children build character to attach to their names since the day they were born. Collecting these good habits and using them often helps them to choose beneficial and productive behaviors over bad and unproductive behaviors without really having to think about it. This means they are also building inner strength that will carry them through stressful and uncertain times as they navigate from childhood into young adults, where parental influence decreases.

> *"Train up a child in the way he should go,*
> *and when he is old he will not depart from it"*

> *— Proverbs 22:6*

DEALING WITH HIGH SCHOOL CLIQUES

As children approach the end of their high school years, adding to and protecting the value of their names can become more difficult. Teenagers tend to clump together in groups, and those groups tend to dislike and even cut down outsiders. While being a part of a group can make your child's life easier and teach them skills like sharing experiences and respecting others, it can also teach them to exclude people who are different or don't fit in or even how to hurt others on purpose with words or actions.

Friendship groups can form around things people have in common, including sports, music, and academic talent. Members of these groups feel a sense of belonging and feel they can be themselves within the group. Some of these groups are flexible about members and will welcome anyone, while others are more restricted and cliquish.

This second type of group normally has a strict code of membership and accepts only certain ways to act. This group focuses on status and popularity rather than shared values and beliefs, which makes it a less desirable group from a parent's perspective.

People in cliques sometimes use their power to hurt others through insults, exclusion and even bullying those who are not perceived to "fit in" due to their looks, economic standing or hobbies. Members of these clique groups end up dealing with a lot of pressures and rules, and tend to constantly worry that they will be dropped from the group.

Parents should monitor their child's interactions with these types of groups carefully because insecure clique members often resort to humiliation, rumors and manipulation to preserve their status in the group. You do not want your child to become the target of this type of behavior.

Be sure to talk with your child and let them know that friendships change and being popular is not the most important thing in life. Encourage them to be friends with all sorts of people and to practice being a good friend by being respectful, fair, trustworthy, honest and caring so that they will attract people with similar traits into their inner circle. Remind them that those are the labels they want to be associated with their name.

Therefore encourage one another and build each other up,
just as in fact you are doing.

1 Thessalonians 5:11

A PERSONAL NOTE:

While growing up, I was friends with kids from several families in our area, two of which were the children of pastors. The one friend, a boy, loved being a preacher's kid, but the other, a girl, hated it.

The girl said that her friends decided that because of her father's job she was a "good girl" and no fun to hang around with, so she wasn't invited to group functions. It was clear to her she had been pre-judged, and she would never get a chance to show she was just like them.

To try to remove the stigma of being a pastor's daughter, she took it to the extreme. She started skipping school, cussing, and drinking in an effort to fit in. Soon, she was out of control.

It got so bad that rumors reached her parents. When they confronted her about it, she became defensive and tried to explain what she was feeling. Her parents didn't want to hear it, and explained that she should not do anything to bring shame to the family. They were more worried their reputation in the community than anything their daughter was going through.

Because of her parents' reaction and lack of understanding, she refused to change her ways. Her behavior continued to spiral out of control and she eventually ended up dropping out of school because she was pregnant.

It wasn't until she was in her early twenties that she finally realized that people in the community did not associate good things with her name. She realized she had a choice: move to a new location where no one knew her and she could rebuild her name into something she could be proud of, or stick it out where she was and prove to everyone that she had grown up and changed her ways. She understood she had to start the journey or the value of her name would never change.

The moral of this story? As parents, we need to listen to what our children are saying to us and acknowledge their feelings — even if what they're feeling and the problems they're facing seem silly or trivial to us. Had the parents in the previous story bothered to listen to their daughter's concerns, the story would have had a much different ending.

FINDING PURPOSE

Your young adult child may have already found their purpose and started on a path leading in that direction, but they may also be feeling lost and unsure of what they'll be doing with their life after high school. If you've been helping your child build his or her name thus far, you have already laid the groundwork and your child has a good foundation. Now it's just time to help them move in a direction that will help them lead a successful and fulfilling life.

Simply asking them, "What is your passion?" might not be enough to move them onto the correct path. Most children this age haven't had enough life experience to figure that out and it puts too much pressure on them. Instead, start them thinking about why they like what they like, what their strengths and values are and how those could fit into possible careers and life goals.

During this initial step, it doesn't matter what their answers are, it's more important to point out that your child has things they care about. For example, if your child likes comic books, you might ask them to research all of the different skills it takes to bringing a comic book to life. This will encourage your child to broaden his or her frame of reference and possibly point them toward future college majors or occupations.

SETTING GOALS

Young people are usually filled with optimism and hope, but those feelings don't always translate to anything meaningful in the real world. Lofty goals and dreams of a "fun" job will not help your child earn a living, so it's up to you to give them a reality check without quashing their dreams.

Sitting down with your child and establishing long- and short-term goals can help them figure out how their actions will impact their future and their name. Parents can share stories of their own experiences, good and bad, to help guide their children.

Parents should also talk about expectations versus reality. Many young people expect to enter the job market at the same level as their parents' current level, and are severely disappointed when they find out that just doesn't happen. Parents should be sure their child realizes that careers take time and a lot of work to build. Discuss some of the steps you took to reach the level you currently hold in your profession and the education or training it took, as well as how many years you've spent in your occupation.

Ultimately, purpose is linked to your child's name, so it is important that you help them decide how they want to make their contribution to the world. So, spend quality time discussing this and really listen to what your child tells you. Then, based upon what they've said, ask them how their interests connect with what is happening in the real world and would this translate to something they might want to pursue in college or as a career. Sometimes, asking the right questions can lead them to the answers they need in order to make an informed decision.

As you are helping your child set goals and decide the path they want to take, it's important to remember that this is their path and you're just there as an advisor and guide. As long as the path isn't completely unrealistic, i.e. planning to become a rock star when the child doesn't play an instrument or sing, or a nuclear physicist when the child has no aptitude for math, you should encourage them to explore the possibilities and trust them to travel their own path.

If you've done a good job building the foundation of your child's name, and taught them its value, they will figure it out for themselves. Just be sure to let them know that you're available for questions, discussions and moral support any time they need it.

THE NEXT BIG STEP

Whether your child plans are to continue their education by going to college or a trade school or go straight into the workforce after graduation, there are things you can do as a parent to help them prepare for the next phase of their lives.

Parents should start involving their child in tasks like scheduling their own doctor's appointments, opening a checking account, monitoring their bank balances, meal planning and grocery shopping, budgeting, doing their own laundry, preparing simple nutritional meals, etc. so that they are more prepared to handle things when they are out on their own or away at school. This means that parents have to be willing to give the child more independence and allow them to possibly fail while they are still in a safe home environment.

It's also important to reinforce the problem-solving skills you've been teaching your child throughout his or her life so that they will be able to handle unexpected challenges. Expand on these skills to include how to get along with a roommate, what to do when they find themselves struggling with a class, and how to balance study time and a social life. Be sure your child is not afraid to ask for help, regardless of the situation, and let them know that doing so does not reflect badly upon them or their name.

CHAPTER 7

Your Name After High School

When I was a child, I used to speak like a child, think like a child, reason like a child; when I became a man, I did away with childish things.

1 Corinthians 13:11

The move from high school to college or vocational school is, for many, the first big step into the adult world. It's also a big step down in social hierarchy. Your child will be going from being a top of the totem pole high school senior to a lowly college freshmen, which is a big adjustment for some.

It's completely normal for children to feel nervous and apprehensive about this time in their lives. What makes it especially difficult for parents is you're going to experience a lot of the same feelings, but for different reasons.

Fear of the unknown will run rampant for both the child and parents for a while. Your nearly adult children are suddenly faced with making big decisions that will have an impact on the rest of their lives, and you are facing the fact your fledgling child is about to leave the nest for the first time. Parents need to put aside their anxieties and help their children as they embark on this next leg of their life journey.

While there are many articles and resources that give details about how to prepare your child to go off to college that deal with academics and building networks of friends and contacts on campus, there aren't nearly as many dealing with the social pressures and dangers that face teens who are out on their own for the first time. These are the things, more than academic performance, that can have a real impact on your child's name.

Parents will be treading a perilous path between granting their teen independence and offering not too stifling support when their child comes to them for advice. But, parents also need to realize that college, especially for freshmen, is a dangerous place.

To give you an idea of just how dangerous we're talking about, read this list of questions ER doctor and public speaker Louis M. Profeta, MD received from college students:

> "…What if I just snorted one Xanax? Can you really soak a tampon in alcohol and get drunk? Is cough syrup okay to mix with vodka? Is ecstasy and molly the same thing? Can't you just strap a backpack to them to keep them from rolling over so they don't choke on their own vomit? What about Phenergan? What's in skittles (not the candy)? How many milligrams of THC can you eat and not die? Are they starting to add stuff to coke (not the cola) that makes you more hyped? How much does it cost to go to an ER and will you call my parents if I go? How can you tell if your roommate is suicidal? What if you know your roommate is using heroin … should I tell their parents? How do I tell if the 'bars' I bought online are not fentanyl? I got raped last year … should I tell someone now? I think my roommate is going to probably kill herself…who do I tell?"

So, now that you're frightened out of your mind and second-guessing your child's college enrollment, consider this additional bit of wisdom from the doctor: "Some of these young men and women are simply too emotionally immature and lack the basic self-control and sense of personal responsibility to be in college." But, if you've done a good job helping your child build a solid foundation and name, then your child isn't one of the ones who aren't ready.

Throughout your child's life, you've help to build their strong character and given them the tools they need to become a successful, independent young adult. You've basically guaranteed that they will be able to function just fine without you, which is truly your goal as a parent.

TEMPTATIONS

Regardless of how well you've prepared your child for life away from you and the safety of home, college students are bombarded by worldly temptations. There will be a lot pressure coming at your child, as well as a lot of things that will require willpower to manage — things like more difficult classes and extended study time, figuring out time management, getting along with roommates, and trying to fit extracurricular activities into their schedule without impacting their grades. Poor impulse control and folding to peer pressure can make your child's college dreams turn into a nightmare if you haven't prepared them adequately to deal with this kind of stress.

Here are a few things to prepare them for:

Peer pressure is just as bad at this stage of life, if not worse than it was in high school. This can be pressure related to anything from skipping class to drugs and sex.

Roommates may be something your child has never had to deal with, let alone living with virtual strangers. This can be challenging, so you should encourage your child to try to get along.

Dealing with multiple changes all at the same time can be overwhelming. This can include new friends, new living conditions, different routines, being away from parental guidance for the first time, possible homesickness and missing friends at home.

Drinking and drugs being more readily available. Parents have to hope that the foundation they built with their child will help them withstand the lure of both of these temptations.

Sex and sexual experimentation are easier when students are away from their parents and adult authority figures. Again, parents should trust that they have raised responsible young adults who, if they decide to engage in sexual activity, will do so safely. A review of safe sex practices and birth control, while possibly embarrassing for all parties, should happen before school starts.

Large parties and gatherings are a given on a college campus. Arming your new college student with these tips is important: the buddy system should always be employed, be constantly aware of surroundings, always pour your own beverages, never leave beverages or food sitting around unattended, always carry a fully charged cell phone, don't give in to peer pressure, don't go anywhere by yourself, don't leave with someone you don't know, know your limits.

Time management issues can sometimes sneak up on students who aren't careful about organizing their classwork around their social calendar. Procrastination and being disorganized can take a toll on grades if students aren't diligent.

Addressing these concerns with your child before they start their college career is beneficial, and will hopefully lower the anxiety level for everyone. Keeping the lines of communication open will go a long way toward your child continuing to protect and build his or her name into something you can both be proud of.

SOCIAL MEDIA AND YOUR NAME

Your young adult's college career does not end efforts to continue building on his or her name. In fact, this is the point where he or she really starts to build an identity and will need to stay vigilant to be sure it's protected.

In today's world, your name's reputation is more important than ever, mainly because it is so easily accessible through social media. Because of this, you need to impress upon your son or daughter just how important it is for them to think carefully before posting on social media. This is because what is seen there can have a huge impact on many areas of their lives for an indeterminate amount of time and reflect either good things or bad things about their name. Here are just a few of the ways:

Nearly all employers check applicants' online presence and social media posts as part of their screening process. Depending on what they find there, the profile and posts could help or disqualify you from your dream job. (One report shows that 70% of HR professionals have denied a candidate due to inappropriate social media content.)

Because this is an important tool to help find a good job, careful planning and posting should be the rule for all social media accounts. Your profiles should also be professional and show you in the best light possible.

The types of followers your account attracts can also impact your perceived value to potential employers, especially if you have influencers or other industry leaders in the group. Being well-connected makes an impact.

Having inactive social media accounts can send the message that you don't know how to engage people. Social media gives you a chance to show your ability to network, engage others and create relevant content. Failing to do so can be a red flag to employers.

Making your social media private can also have a negative effect. If potential employers cannot find you online, they might think that either you have something to hide or nothing to show for yourself — either can send your resume to the bottom of the pile.

A well-managed social media presence can demonstrate leadership, critical thinking and problem-solving skills.

Social media can influence bank lenders. Banks are starting to look at social media profiles when making lending decisions. Lenders might view your profiles to validate employment, confirm identity, and look for red flags that might indicate irresponsible spending or fraud. Something as simple as misspelled words and grammatical errors or typing posts in all caps might be interpreted as lack of education or earning power. It's also possible that lenders might assume that friends' behaviors will mirror your own, since people tend to befriend like-minded people — again pointing to careful monitoring of who follows your accounts.

Your profiles can say a lot about your employability. A LinkedIn profile, for example, can reflect job stability or lack thereof, as well as how seriously you take your career path. This type of profile can act almost as a resume for potential employers, as well as giving lending institutions an idea of your employment history. Therefore, it's important to have a complete profile that shows education, job experience, and the number of times you've switched jobs and whether it was a move up, down or merely a lateral move. It would also be a good idea to seek recommendations from colleagues.

As you can see, social media has become a huge part of our everyday lives, so the above advice isn't just for children and young adults. Adults need to be just a mindful of their online presence so that they can protect their names as well. Everyone should also be aware that social media never dies and can come back to haunt you years later. This is the best reason why monitoring your accounts and posting carefully should start early.

FROM HIGH SCHOOL STRAIGHT TO THE JOB MARKET
College or vocational school isn't the only path your young adult can choose after graduating from high school. Some may decide that the lure of earning their own money and enjoying the independence that allows is the way they want to step into adulthood.

The rising cost of education may also play a large role in choosing to jump straight in to the job market. Many young adults and their parents don't want to shoulder the huge debt required to earn a college or vocational school degree. This decision will put them in a much better position debt to earnings-wise than their college graduate peers, who are burdened by student loans as soon as they leave school.

For parents who had high hopes of their child graduating from college, take heart. Many times, entering the workforce straight after high school helps the young adult make a better decision about schooling in the future. Being in the job market helps them to learn what they're truly interested in pursuing. They will have also learned responsibility, how to connect and work with others, how to dress and act appropriately for the job, how to be a team player, and how to balance their work and social life — all of which will give them an advantage over recent college grads.

Regardless of the path your young adult chooses, they will be taking with them all of the name-building tools you, as parents and caregivers, provided them as they were growing up. As they take this first step into independence, they will be able to rely on the foundation you helped them to build for their name, and will hopefully continue to maintain and polish it.

CONCLUSION

When your child is a young adult, it can take a lot of work for them to continue to be a person of integrity and keep building on their name. It's the parents' job to remind them that doing this will make them stand out. They should also be made aware that they will probably have to make sacrifices and at times go against their friends and peers to keep this good standing.

While this might be difficult for them, in the end doing this will give them the ability to be strong and focused as they start to navigate their life as an adult. Their name has so much more value during these years than they might realize, and as parents it's your job to help them navigate these final steps before adulthood.

"A good name is to be chosen
rather than great riches, loving favor
rather than silver and gold."

— Proverbs 22:1

CHAPTER 8

Your Name as an Adult and in the Workforce

A person's good reputation, his name, is his most valuable asset. Indeed, the Bible shows that God guards and protects His name very jealously. This is because His name represents what He is.

— The Soncino Commentary

The good habits developed as children and teens will directly connect to our name as we become adults. But, just because you've become an adult, doesn't mean you can stop building and continuously protecting your name. Your name, i.e. reputation, is just as important now as it has ever been, and being aware of how easily it can be shattered is important. Reputation, which comes from the Latin word *reputationem*, means "consideration." So, your name's reputation dictates how people consider or label you — good or bad.

Your name determines the way you are viewed by society. You are constantly judged on your name, it's talked about and people will make their own judgments as to whether it's got a good association or a bad one. They will look at your character, the way you communicate and whether you can be trusted.

As you navigate the adult world, you need to be aware that your name can become tarnished easily as situations and circumstances change, so you must remain vigilant. Sometimes, just one negative complaint or opinion can start to erode all the hard work you've done to ensure your name is in good standing.

Your name should be a natural outgrowth of you striving to be

the person you most want to be.

YOUR NAME AT WORK

What does your name say about you professionally? When we start our professional journey, it is understood by most that we are still learning our profession and do not have a name in the professional field yet.

In most cases, you keep your job or lose it based on the performance you demonstrate, and your performance has your name attached to it. If you get promoted, it's because you have impressed the leadership of your organization through your actions and the perceived value your name has for the organization.

Therefore, having a good name at work is a powerful asset that can make you stand out from your colleagues. Your name can also affect the types of job offers you receive, especially when hiring managers see your good work ethic and consistently exemplary performance.

In today's highly-competitive workplace, your name is even more important than it has been in the past, because in business your name is the only currency that matters. Therefore, you cannot just coast along on the work you've done to build your name in the past, you must continuously work to keep your name in good standing with your boss, coworkers, customers and the world at large.

"If I take care of my character, my reputation will take care of me."

— Dwight L. Moody

PERCEPTION

One of the most controlling factors in your life and how it relates to your name is how you are perceived by others. The integrity and character of your name are critical to your career. Striving to have your name associated with being consistent, leading by example and not compromising will help you go far in your chosen field.

To help attach the perception you want to your name at work, consider the following:

- Be on time.

- Meet all deadlines.

- Do what you say you're going to do (be dependable).

- Be decisive.

- Be effective and efficient.

- Be flexible.

- Be constantly learning to make future work better.

- Be honest with yourself and others, and always think through why you did and said what you did.

- Be sincere with people and avoid trying to "spin" things in your favor.

- Be humble.

- Take ownership of mistakes.

- Be generous.

- Be interested in those around you.

- Be resilient.

- Be proactive with problem solving

- Listen and ask for the views of others.

- Share responsibility and credit.

Doing all of these things will help others think of your name in a good way every time they work with you, plus your name will stand out when superiors are looking for someone to promote.

Look for these things in your work life to indicate people respect your name: they ask you for advice, they welcome your feedback, you get recognized for your efforts, and leaders ask you to participate in new projects often because of the trust you have built. All of these things indicate you have built a name that indicates knowledge, intelligence, diligence, hard work/great work ethic and reliability. If, on the other hand, you're seeing the exact opposite reactions pop up often in your work life, then you need to work on polishing your name (see chapter ?? for help with this).

Your strong name in the business world can also do things like:

- Attract better opportunities

- Allow you to command a higher salary

- Give you opportunities for leadership roles

- Create a competitive advantage over your fellow employees

Your name's perception is likely your greatest intangible asset. When you are seen as reliable, responsible and trustworthy, you have set yourself apart from your fellow employees and have given yourself a great advantage in the workplace.

> *"You can't buy a good reputation; you must earn it."*
>
> — *Harvey Mackay*

PERSONAL STORY:

I have been in a supervisory position more than once during my career, and I know that when I was interviewing candidates for job openings there was almost always a conversation like this:

Upper management to middle managers at a staff meeting: "Okay, everyone, please listen up. We have a leadership position opening up in the next quarter. Are there any current employees that might be a good fit for the position?"

Someone will usually speak up and say something like: "John Turner and Barbra Spencer are good candidates. They have both been with us for more than ten years, and have filled in as supervisor when needed. They both have a good work ethic and reputations for being punctual."

Notice how this manager associated only good things with both of these people's names? This is the way you can leverage your name into a promotion, by being sure that only good things are associated with it. The conversation would have been a bit different if the two employees' names weren't quite as equally good. Consider this scenario:

They both have ten years of experience, do exemplary work and are punctual. The difference is, one is polite, respectful and well-liked by management and fellow employees, but the other is opinionated and rude, and management and his coworkers don't care for him. There are worries that this employee will be too stubborn to take direction or consider other viewpoints when problem-solving. That, coupled with his inability to get along with coworkers, makes him the loser in this contest.

While both can perform the job, the perception of their names helped decide which would be better for the job.

The moral of this story is: remember that people's perception of you comes from multiple sources, i.e. everything you do and say. People do not form their opinions of your name based solely on the good things you do, they also consider the not so good things, and those things, unfortunately for you, almost always carry more weight.

"Decide what you want your reputation in the workplace to be and let your actions define you."

— Reba Hull Campbell

YOUR NAME AND APPEARANCE IN THE WORKPLACE

In today's world, we aren't supposed to judge people by their appearance. In reality, that can't always be the case. If you are a behind a scenes employee, your appearance and mode of dress more than likely won't impact your job. On the other hand, if you deal with the public regularly, your look may have a significant impact on your future.

You could be the most conscientious, dedicated employee ever, but if you have piercings, tattoos and dress in a non-traditional way while working for a company whose clientele is mostly conservative, you probably aren't going to be as successful as your coworkers who don't have body art and wear business attire. In this case, people's perceptions of something you chose to do with body modification and dress style count for more than your good job performance.

For those who think it's an individual's right to dress and modify their body as the want, consider this information on perception from a study cited in the *Journal of Police and Criminal Psychology*:

> There is an ongoing debate whether police officers should be allowed to wear tattoos or piercings on visible parts of the body or not. One argument says such body modifications would cue negative evaluations of officers by citizens that would impede officers' fulfillment of their duties. ...
>
> The present research aims to close this gap by examining how citizens perceive police officers with tattoos and piercings. In an experiment, participants saw edited photographs of police officers with and without tattoos (study 1) or piercings (study 2). They rated each officer regarding communion, agency, likability, respect, and threat.
>
> We found that, as expected, police officers with tattoos and piercings were perceived as less trustworthy and less competent, were liked somewhat less, and triggered higher perceptions of threat. In addition, police officers with tattoos (but not with piercings) were perceived as less friendly and more assertive.

Whether we like it or not, we all have perceptions of people based upon both their looks and their actions. If you want to work for a company whose clientele, and even management, have obvious negative perceptions about certain things like body modification and trendy clothing styles, then you should avoid those things being associated with your name to help you succeed while employed there. If, on the other hand, you want to work for an upscale tattoo shop, then body modifications and quirky clothing would be an asset to the perception of your name.

This reality might be difficult to adjust to for young adults just entering the workforce, especially if they're coming straight from a college atmosphere where wild and flamboyant personal expression in all forms was applauded and carried no negative consequences.

Emerging from the self-absorbed and entitled bubble these young adults existed in during their school years and entering corporate America is a big culture shock. They must learn quickly what the norms and rules are for the environment where they want to be employed, and realize explicitly how and why these rules and expectations are different from what was expected of them when they were in school.

In order to succeed, these young professionals have to be willing to make the effort to transition to this new environment. This can include recognizing which skills they lack, reaching out to older employees for direction, etc. and ultimately realizing they are solely responsible for making this transition and should not expect leniency from their employer (and customers) if they are not completely successful.

A tough lesson to learn is: You don't *deserve* anything you haven't worked hard to get. Whether it is money, items, jobs, promotions or even love — all must be earned.

"The most important thing that parents can teach their children

is how to get along without them."

—Frank A. Clark

CHAPTER 9

Your Name and Forming Adult Friendships

If either of them falls down, one can help the other up. But pity anyone who falls and has no one to help them up.

— Ecclesiastes 4:10

At the beginning of an adult relationship, we are usually on our best behavior and work very hard to make a good impression on a new person or group we are interested in becoming a part of. We want to be "liked" and included in activities or romantic pursuits.

By deciding that we want to be included with this group or person, we have already formed opinions about what they believe, how they act and what they expect. What we mustn't forget is these romantic interests and groups also have expectations and have already formed opinions about us.

This is another instance where a well-maintained name is extremely important. While you could pretend to be better than the name you've earned for yourself, that will only last so long. Eventually, your true name will become known. No one likes to be fooled, so representing your authentic self and showing people who you are is key to building new relationships of any kind.

So, as long as you have been working to keep your name polished and clean, you have nothing to worry about when you show people exactly who you are. If, however, your name has some tarnish, then you might need to do some extra work to bring it back to what it should be (see chapter ??).

The concept of keeping your name as polished and stain-free as possible is so important in our society now that reputation management companies have started to become popular. These companies are paid to help you police your name, both socially and online, to make sure your name stays as pristine as possible. This type of business might become even more relevant as the majority of us continue to post our lives on social media for everyone to see, and ultimately judge us for what we're doing.

FORMING FRIENDSHIPS

While we all hope to leave our high school years behind, many of the behaviors we saw then are still happening in our adult life. For example, if you decide to befriend someone who has a name associated with not so good things, then you will be tarnishing your name by association. So, just like when your parents cautioned you about hanging out with certain people in high school, you now have to police your relationships.

Friendship is too valuable a resource to spend on unworthy people. Plus, you've worked hard to make your name something you can be proud of, and you don't want to associate with people who will drag your name down with theirs.

You've heard the saying, "birds of a feather flock together"? Whether that's true or not, the public perception is that it's true. Your name's reputation will be reflected through your friends, and give people ideas about what you are most likely all about.

At this point in your life, you should be socially developed enough to choose friends who will enhance your name rather than bring it down. While friends don't have to see eye to eye on everything, they should share the same morals and values, otherwise you'll most likely find yourself in situations you do not want to be in.

It can be more daunting to make friends as an adult, partially because your life is busier and there are more demands on your time, but also because you realize that a true friend, rather than just an acquaintance, is difficult to find. When looking for friends as an adult, look for the following:

- Integrity
- Trust
- Honesty
- Dependability
- Loyalty
- Empathy
- Good listening skills
- Confidence
- Sense of humor
- Non-judgmental
- Low maintenance
- Fun to be around

When you find someone whose name ticks all or nearly all of those boxes for you, you've found someone who could become a true friend. Just be sure your name does the same for them, because they are looking for the same things from a friend that you are.

> *One who has unreliable friends soon comes to ruin,*
> *but there is a friend who sticks closer than a brother.*
> — Proverbs 18:24

CHAPTER 10

Your Name
and Adult Dating

Mature love is composed and sustaining;
a celebration of commitment, companionship, and trust.

— H. Jackson Brown, Jr.

Dating as an adult is more challenging than when you were in high school or even college. It's more difficult to meet someone organically because your social circles have broadened and you are more likely to be faced with many people you barely know or don't know at all. Your focus has also most likely changed, as has your level of maturity. You're probably looking for more meaningful and rewarding relationships at this point in your life.

Just as you were looking for specific things from friendship, you're going to look for similar things from a romantic partner. These things include honesty, trust, respect and open communication, as well as the ability to compromise.

Romantic relationships are another area where the value placed on your name is extremely important. Anyone who intends to involve themselves with you on that level will want to know what they're getting into and they will use your name to help them determine that.

While we are almost always on our best behavior when trying to impress someone, as the saying goes, "you can't put lipstick on a pig" and pretend it's a beautiful woman. The same goes for your name. You can't just pretend that your name isn't tarnished or disguise that tarnish as something else. If you truly want a relationship with the person, then it's best to be open and honest about everything. Each person looking for a romantic relationship is ultimately asking themselves, "Is this person worth my time and energy?"

Knowing what kind of life you want to live, as well as knowing what type of partner you want to be, will help make genuine connections that will lead to better relationships. The lesson to learn here is: the best way to find an amazing partner is to become an amazing partner.

HELP FINDING AN AMAZING PARTNER

To become that amazing partner, you will need to take a close look at how you've dealt with relationships in the past, and then improve your "game." Your name can be stellar, but you can still be lacking in the areas needed for good romantic relationships.

Some things to work on and look for when searching for a meaningful relationship include:

Neediness. This means you place a higher priority on what others think of you than what you think of yourself. This can show up in your behavior as altering your words or actions to fit someone else's needs rather than your own. Doing this can come off as desperate and it's a major turn-off. No one wants a relationship with someone who isn't genuine.

An example would be a needy person tries to impress a date by talking about how much money they make or how many celebrities they know or what fancy college they attended, rather than just getting to know the person and seeing if their interests are compatible.

The solution to this problem is to care more about what you think of yourself than what others think.

Take care of yourself. No one can see the value of your name if you don't value it yourself. The value of your name should include caring for your health, finances, career and social life to be sure that all of these areas of your life reflect the value of your name. All of these areas take time and effort to maintain and you never really get to stop working on them. The goal is to work towards having your name be the best version of itself at all times.

• **Communicate.** Rather than trying to find tactics and strategies or even the perfect "formula" for finding a romantic partner, you should be a mature, functioning adult who can communicate and express yourself honestly.

• **Vulnerability.** Don't view being vulnerable as "giving the other person all the power" in your relationship, or as a tactic to get what you want. Being vulnerable and expressing your desires, and being willing to accept the consequences related to them — good or bad — is an attractive trait. By doing this, you're saying "this is who I am" and if you don't like me, then I'm okay with that.

• **Emotional baggage.** Most adults have had previous relationships, and that's okay. It's pretty much impossible to find someone who doesn't have some emotional baggage. The key is to find someone who can see their own flaws and be accountable for them, but not controlled by them. Having open conversations about this baggage, with no blaming or shaming, is difficult but will help you to find a healthy long-term relationship. The only way this works is to express things with honesty, integrity and rather than blame, shame and game-playing.

• **Excitement.** Is the person you're with someone who makes you excited to be with them? If both people involved aren't excited about the relationship, then it's doomed to fail. If this is to be a long-term relationship, then both of you need to be on board and excited about each major step you take together, despite any apprehensions either of you might have — from dating to fighting with each other to getting married to buying a car, etc.

In conclusion, to have the best chance at success in the relationship game, be the best version of your name, unapologetically and without shame. Doing this will attract like-minded people to you who will connect on your level. This will also help you weed out those with undesirable names who will waste your time and possibly tarnish your name in the process.

⁴Love is patient and kind; love does not envy or boast;

it is not arrogant ⁵or rude.

It does not insist on its own way; it is not irritable or resentful;

⁶it does not rejoice at wrongdoing, but rejoices with the truth.

⁷Love bears all things, believes all things, hopes all things,

endures all things.

— 1 Corinthians 13:4-7

CHAPTER 11

Your Name and Marriage

Neither man nor woman is perfect or complete without the other.
Thus, no marriage or family, no ward or stake is likely to reach its full
potential until husbands and wives,
mothers and fathers, men and women work together in unity of purpose,
respecting and relying upon each other's strengths.

— Sheri L. Dew

E veryone talks about finding the "right" person when speaking about marriage, but in reality, *you* have to be the right person. Do you know who you are, where you came from, where you're going, what your strengths and weaknesses are, and which behaviors you'd like to improve? If you don't know yourself, then it's difficult to find someone to share your life.

We all have vulnerabilities and blind spots, but having the ability to recognize this and work on these issues within ourselves is key to continuing to build our names into something we can be proud of so that we can attract a spouse who will be with us for the long haul.

To better understand your views on what a marriage should be, talk to your parents, grandparents and other relatives about their marriage experiences. Ask them what they think makes a good marriage and also what they think makes a marriage fail. I'm sure their answers will tell you that relationships require a lot of mutual trust and vulnerability.

DEALING WITH CONFLICT

Conflicts inevitably happen in long-term relationships. Hopefully you have enough self-awareness to avoid behaving in ways that make your partner defensive when this happens. Blaming, oversimplifying and playing the victim is not the way to deal with conflict. Marriage is not a "one wins/one loses" proposition when disagreements occur. Instead, you and your spouse should work together to evaluate the problem and find a solution or compromise, depending on the situation, that works for both of you.

No one ever said that marriage was easy — it takes skill to be successful. While that doesn't sound romantic in the least, it is necessary. For a couple to be happy in marriage, they must be able to understand what their partner is saying and also know their partner's experience that's fueling the words. In other words, if you can't put yourself in your partner's shoes empathetically, then all the communication in the world won't help.

Having a healthy marriage means having skills for conflict resolution. Here are a few habits to get into that will help you along the way:

- **Know yourself.** Know how you react when you are upset and work to communicate calmly and reasonably instead of closing yourself off or yelling. Also, take a look at past arguments and how you reacted in negative ways.

- **Don't jump to conclusions.** Give your spouse the benefit of the doubt rather than acting skeptical, because doing that will make your spouse defensive, anxious or even angry. Acting skeptical gives your partner the impression that you are judging them unfairly. You cannot resolve a conflict if you've already made up your mind.

- **Pick your battles.** Learn to distinguish between what can be overlooked and what needs to be addressed. You can preserve pace by choosing to overlook the little annoyances and slights. There is no need to start a war over something that is small in the grand scheme of things.

- **See the bigger picture.** Arguments and tension are most often the expressions of frustration and possibly deeper problems. Take a step back and look at what's going on in your life and your spouse's life, then cut each other some slack when needed.

- **Don't bring up old fights.** Stick to the issue at hand and don't be in the habit of bringing up old grievances. Doing this will distract you from finding a resolution to the current conflict. Plus, bring up old wounds and baggage will most likely spark another conflict.

- **Don't brood on it.** It's unwise to dwell on conflict and stew about your anger and frustration. Even the bible says, "Be ye angry, and sin not: let not the sun go down upon your wrath." Ephesians 4:26. Trying to ignore or put off a conflict can lead to bitterness and resentment, and that is not the way you want to go.

- **Give grace, and then give it again.** In other words, show kindness and understanding to someone else, even when they're irritating you. Doing this will oftentimes help you avoid conflict altogether.

As a couple, you and your significant other will continue to be two separate people, but you will also be tied to each other in various ways, including how your name as a couple is viewed by those in the outside world. I'm sure you don't want your couple's name to be associated with "always arguing" or "can't compromise" or "that toxic duo", so finding and practicing good conflict resolution habits should be on your list of things to do to keep your relationship on track and happy.

Be kind to one another, tender-hearted, forgiving each other,

just as God in Christ also has forgiven you.

— Ephesians 4:32

CHAPTER 12

Your Name
and Being a Grandparent

*"A grandparent is a little bit parent,
a little bit teacher, and a little bit best friend."*

Grandparent can be another addition to the name you've built for yourself. This can be an enjoyable and rewarding addition to your name or it can be a disappointing struggle — you get to decide which it will be based upon your actions and attitude.

While it can be tempting to be the "Santa Claus" grandparent who gives the grandchildren everything their hearts desire, that isn't the best thing for them, you or their parents. Contradicting the house rules your grandchildren's parents have established is confusing for the children and can wreck all the hard work that's been done to build their names as responsible rule followers — not to mention causing conflict between you and their parents.

Butting heads with parenting styles is one of the biggest complaints noted by both parents and grandparents in the C.S. Mott Children's Hospital National Poll on Children's Health conducted by Michigan Medicine. The disagreements cited included parents thinking grandparents were too lenient/strict, conflicts about how to discipline, what foods were served to children and amount of screen time or TV allowed.

As a grandparent, you will need to be respectful of the house rules your grandchildren are expected to follow and continue those rules in your home. While you might not agree with some or even all of the rules, keeping things consistent will make the experience more enjoyable for everyone involved and earn you more time with your grandchildren.

Of course, you want to add loving and caring grandparent to the list of qualities attached to your name. You should want to be there to help with developing your grandchildren's cognitive skills, identity, self-esteem and knowledge of family history. It's also okay to be the one your grandchildren voice their concerns to, and you can be compassionate and forgiving when they come to you with their problems. Doing this can make the relationship deeply meaningful and pleasurable for both you and your grandchildren.

Today's grandparents can be an important resource for parents and grandchildren, as long as grandparents remember that parents are the ones in charge of raising the children. As a grandparent, your role is to fit in with the existing family culture, and allow the parents to delegate authority to you when they deem necessary. In other words, you had your chance to raise your children, now you need to have faith that you did a good job and that they know what they're doing as they raise their own children.

COMMUNICATION

Criticizing or judging the parenting style of your adult child and how they handle various situations can undermine their authority with their children. So, keeping an open mind is important. Learn why things are done the way they're done in your adult child's household and then adopt their house rules as your own.

If you have suggestions if your input is welcome. If it's not, then you should keep things to yourself — even if you think what's being done is a big mistake. Unless it's life threatening, you have to let your adult children make their own parenting mistakes so they can learn from them.

In order to see grandchildren often, grandparents need to cultivate a good relationship with their adult child (the parent) so that they will facilitate additional visits. If there are constant disagreements over house rules, discipline, etc. parents are less likely to encourage frequent visits. Finding a way to effectively communicate and establishing harmony between the two households will mean seeing your grandchildren more often. It will also mean your adult child includes supportive, loving, and helpful when thinking of your name.

EXPECTATIONS

If you do it right, you will have an extremely important role in your grandchildren's lives. Be the grandparent who consistently follows the family rules and doesn't confuse children's ideas of who is in charge, but still makes visits fun and exciting for the grandchildren.

You definitely do not want visits with you to be something your grandchildren feel they "have" to do. You should make sure they don't feel uncomfortable, bored or confused by conflicting rules when they visit. Your grandchildren should look forward to seeing you, because you're one of the few adults in their lives who has lots of time for them and makes things fun.

Find interesting and entertaining ways to impart family history, play games, find common interests or start a hobby together, be a role model and become a spiritual guide by introducing them to the wonders of nature or engaging in acts of charity. Doing these things will guarantee they associate acceptance, supportive, patience, love, safe harbor, stability and wisdom, along with fun and adventure with your name.

BENEFITS FOR YOU

A close relationship with your grandchildren can be beneficial to your health, as well as your mind and emotions. Becoming an active and supportive grandparent can also make you feel more energy, optimism and sense of purpose, as well as making you feel more youthful as you get to play like a child again when you interact with them. Recent studies have also shown the emotional closeness between grandparent/grandchild helps to protect the older adult against depression and gives a boost to brain function, which can lead to a longer life.

"Children's children are a crown to the aged,
and parents are the pride of their children."
— Proverbs 17:6

PROTECTING YOUR NAME FROM OUTSIDE INFLUENCES

CHAPTER 13

Your Name and Bullies

The people who are bullying you,
they're insecure about who they are, and that's why they're bullying you. It
never has to do with the person they're bullying.
They desperately want to be loved and be accepted,
and they go out of their way to make people feel unaccepted
so that they're not alone.

— Madelaine Petsch

Bullies come from all walks of life and economic statuses, they can be male or female and they are destroyers of self-esteem. Bullying can happen to you at any age and can impact your life in multiple ways.

While society seems to worry most about bullying during childhood, adult bullying is just as prevalent.

At its most basic level, bullying is intentionally and repeatedly causing someone discomfort or harm. People who are bullied usually can't defend themselves, either because they aren't in a position of power or because they are physically weak.

There are many types of bullying, some include:

Physical Bullying — This is the most overt type of bullying behavior. It involves physical harm to body or possessions and can take the form of hitting, tripping, pushing, kicking, pinching or damaging personal property. This type of bullying usually involves a person or group that is stronger or larger than the victim. Males are more likely to be physical bullies than females. The effects of this type of bullying are physical harm and psychological effects like low self-esteem, anxiety and depression.

Verbal Bullying — This type of bullying involves saying or writing mean things about someone. It can include name-calling, insults, threats, teasing, intimidation, inappropriate sexual comments, rumors, racist remarks, etc. This type of bullying, according to studies, is most prevalent in grade school age boys, but can occur at any age with any gender. While this type of bullying can appear to be harmless, it can escalate quickly and cause emotional distress and anxiety.

Social Bullying — This type of bullying can be difficult to recognize, but can end up harming someone's reputation (name) or relationships. This might involve leaving someone out on purpose, telling people not to be friends with the victim, spreading rumors, and intentionally embarrassing the victim in public. This type of bullying is sometimes referred to as "mean girl" or "queen bee" bullying, even though both males and females can perpetrate it. This type of bullying can lead to depression, isolation, extreme loneliness and social anxiety.

Cyber Bullying — This type of bullying can be overt or covert, since it entails behaviors through computers and smartphones. Because of the nature of technology, this bullying can occur at any time, day or night, leaving the victim constantly exposed. Cyberbullying can include abusive or threatening texts and/or emails, direct messages, social media posts, comments on social media posts, deliberately excluding a person online and spreading rumors online. This type of bullying has become more and more prevalent as social media popularity increases and everyone has a smartphone. Cyberbullying can be particularly harmful because it can be constant and follow the victim everywhere. It can cause anxiety, depression, social isolation and self-esteem issues.

Workplace Bullying — This type of bullying has become more common as the world becomes increasingly available online. The Workplace Bullying Institute estimates that nearly 30% of adult workers (76 million people it the US) have been bullied in the workforce. This type of bullying can target a group or a single person and usually includes verbal abuse and intimidation over a length of time. It can cause employees to receive unfavorable treatment and lead to humiliation. The bully can be a manager, supervisor, coworker or subordinate. The impact on the victim can be long-term physical and mental health issues, anxiety, stress, loss of self-esteem and self-doubt.

Prejudicial Bullying — This bullying targets ethnicity, race, religion and sexual orientation. It generally involves the belief that marginalized populations are lesser than others. This type of bullying usually comes from peers. The effects of prejudicial bullying can be anxiety, feelings of worthlessness and isolation.

Sexual Bullying — This type of bullying can be done through technology like emails, direct messaging, texts, etc. as well as face to face. It involves using sexual name-calling, spreading rumors of a sexual nature, making inappropriate jokes, sharing intimate photos/videos, and touching, grabbing, or groping someone without permission. This is possibly the most prevalent type of bullying. Studies have found that 81% of women and 43% of men have experience it in some form. This type of bullying can lead to severe depression, social anxiety and trust issues.

WHAT MAKES A BULLY

Bullies are normally those who suffer from low self-esteem and experience feelings of envy and jealousy that push them to project their own feelings of inadequacy onto their bullying victims so they can deny anything is wrong with themselves. This person is using his or her power over the victim to satisfy psychological shortcomings. Because this feeling doesn't last, they will bully again and again. Bullies often feel that the rules don't apply to them and that those they are bullying deserve what they're getting.

The most insidious bully works to put the victim in his or her place by minimizing or even destroying the victim's name (reputation) to make themselves feel superior. Bullies can come in all ages, races, religions and ethnicities. They can also be institutions you respect, like the government, your church, or other organization.

DEALING WITH BULLIES

Bullies are generally looking for a reaction, so don't give them one. Stay calm, look confident and don't show the bully you are afraid or that your feelings are hurt. Don't fight back if the bullying is physical, since that can make the situation worse.

Being a victim of bullying is stressful and embarrassing. Your first reaction might be to retaliate, but instead you should remain calm and avoid giving the bully what they want — power over you and the thrill of seeing your emotional reaction. Also, rebuttals can often trigger escalating bullying behavior and cause you even more embarrassment and damage to your name.

Most bullies are also cowards, so if you feel safe doing so, confront the bully and ask them to stop doing whatever bullying behavior they've been perpetrating against you. Be sure to stay calm and keep your emotions in control. Again, you don't want to reward the bully with what they want — your emotional reaction.

Definitely don't make threats or inflammatory comments of your own, since that will just make things escalate. You do not want to make the problem bigger than it already is.

If you don't feel this has resolved the issue, you should report the incident to the proper authorities. This can be a parent, teacher, principal, professor, work supervisor, lawyer or the police. When dealing with social media bullying, you can also report, flag or request removal of defamatory/bullying content to the platform where it occurred.

PROTECTING YOUR NAME FROM BULLIES

When a bully threatens the hard work you've done to make your name represent only positive things, talking to people about what has happened is a good first step to start repairing the damage. Be frank about what happened and let people know in a calm and respectful way that the rumors, etc. are not true.

Don't get defensive, just state facts that back up your side of things and leave it at that. You have worked hard to let people know just what your name means, so they will be willing to believe you based upon what they already know about you. Be aware that you might not be able to change some people's thinking, and that's okay.

Continue to do the things you've been doing so that you can disprove the bully's lies through your actions. Showing everyone exactly who the bully is can be the best way to feel vindicated, and might just help prevent them from successfully bullying someone else.

"All cruelty springs from weakness."

— Seneca, 4BC-AD65

CHAPTER 14

Your Name and
Social Media

"Character is like a tree and reputation like its shadow. The shadow is what we think of it; the tree is the real thing."

— Abraham Lincoln

Nearly everyone uses social media today. Twitter, Instagram, Tumblr, Facebook, Vine, Pinterest, YouTube, LinkedIn and many other apps and websites have worked their way into our everyday lives. So, it's important to learn how to protect your name online.

First and foremost, don't post things that can hurt your name professionally. Potential employers, schools, colleges and other organizations now routinely check social media for information. Don't let something you posted hurt your future endeavors. A good rule of thumb is: if you don't want friends, family, classmates, etc. to know something, then don't post it!

While it takes some of the fun and spontaneity out of posting, you should always be aware of how your posts will be viewed by others in your life. Once it's out there, it's very difficult to completely delete it. Consider the University of Oklahoma's quarterback whose tweets made when he was 14 and 15 years old came back to haunt him after he won the Heisman Trophy, or Camilla Cabello's racist Twitter thread. They aren't the only ones being haunted by past posts. CEOs and leaders from media, tech and politics are resigning amid accusations of past racism or bias, and colleges are rescinding admissions when offensive social media posts emerge. No one is exempt!

Damage to your name is the number-one risk from social media according a Global Risk Management's survey. Just one inappropriate tweet can go viral and ruin your reputation. Thus, failing to police yourself can cost you big time — you could lose out on a job you just applied for, be fired from your current job, lose everyone's trust, and see all the hard work you've done to establish your name as a good thing be destroyed by 140 characters.

Remember, your social media posts are there forever — they never truly disappear because people can copy and share them, so deleting them from your account just isn't enough.

TIPS TO PROTECT YOUR NAME
- Always be your best self.
- Don't share personal information or post things that might harm you or other people.
- Be aware of what is public.
- Don't get into arguments on social media.
- Be vigilant in checking posts of others to be sure they aren't posting things about you.
- Check your privacy settings control who can see your information and posts.
- Be careful sharing location. Doing this can let others know where you are, which is both a personal safety issue and a potential issue of you are out at a bar or doing something that will tarnish your name.
- Ask friends, coworkers, etc. to refrain from tagging you in photos and posts.

- Don't post provocative or inappropriate photos or memes.
- Don't post about alcohol or drug use.
- Limit friends and followers to people you know.
- Monitor posts from others when you're tagged in them.
- Most importantly, think twice before you make a post and *never* post when you're angry.

"Why risk shattering your reputation with a moment of thoughtlessness?"
— Jon Michail, Personal & Business Brand Authority Coach

And, although there are times when our reputations are tainted due to the dishonesty of others, God wants us to live in such a way that those who know us won't believe the slander.

— James 1:27

DAMAGE CONTROL

CHAPTER 15

Rebuilding Your Name

"It takes 20 years to build a reputation and five minutes to ruin it. If you think about that, you'll do things differently."

— Warren Buffett

When you realize that the name you've built for yourself isn't what you want it to be, it's time to do damage control. While this won't be an easy task, it can be done.

Start by realize that some people won't forget your past bad name, regardless of how well you rebuild it into something good. Fortunately, with time, most people will only remember the new you.

It will be helpful to make a list of all of the things you think you need to change, as well as those things you've heard others say about you in a negative way. Once that's done, make a plan to address each of these things that will help to reverse perceptions about how your name is associated with them. These things could include:

TURN A NEGATIVE INTO A POSITIVE

Take an honest look at the issues with your name's reputation and see if you can turn that negative into a positive. For example, if you're known for being impatient, turn that around by making it a self-reflection tool. Impatience is often an indication of boredom or lack of enjoyment of a specific activity. So, use this opportunity to investigate what you truly want to do. Finding what you truly want to do or love to do will help to engage your mind and make you find the patience to enjoy it.

Do good deeds. The best way to improve the way people perceive your name is through your actions. This is not a quick fix and only works if you do these good deeds consistently to allow people to establish a new way of thinking about your name.

Volunteer. Giving your time to help others is a great way to add polish to your name. There are many deserving groups that could use your help, including animal shelters, nursing homes, churches, etc. This needs to be a committed effort to helping people, not just you trying to slap a band-aide on your name.

> *"The reputation of a thousand years*
> *may be undermined by the conduct of one hour."*
> — Japanese Proverb

REPAIRING YOUR NAME AT WORK

After making a mistake or many mistakes at work, realize that repairing the damage can be challenging. Not only do you have to be conscientious and try to do flawless work, you also have to overcome the negative perceptions of your coworkers and management.

So, why exactly is it important to have a good reputation at work? There are many reasons, including making your job easier because you get more cooperation from everyone you work with, it can also help you advance or make you look more appealing to prospective employers if you decide to look for a different job.

Other benefits include deeper and more valuable professional relationships and the ability to collaborate more successfully, plus you will have a sense of job security that can make it easier for you to focus on producing your best work and generate creative ideas that might otherwise not happen if you are stressed about job security.

There are a few steps to help repair your work name, but they will require some dedicated effort and a willingness on your part to make some necessary changes.

Accountability: When you make a mistake at work (and in other parts of your life too), you should take responsibility for it rather than blaming others. This will help especially if you've had problems in the past with issues related to your poor judgment. Taking responsibility for your actions and acknowledging the impact of your mistakes can help others recognize your sincerity about changing and possibly move you one step closer to trust from your coworkers and supervisors.

Apologize: When you take responsibility, be sure to apologize for past mistakes and shortcomings. You can go so far as to speak privately with individuals you have wronged or express your feelings in a meeting, depending on the magnitude of your transgressions. This will let your colleagues know that you're willing to accept how your actions impact others, and hopefully they will forgive you.

Make a commitment. Admitting you're wrong and saying you're sorry is not enough. You must make a commitment to learn from your mistakes and grow in your work role. To cement this commitment, you can ask for feedback from your coworkers and supervisors so that you learn their perspectives and better understand what you need to do to overcome future challenges. Take the initiative to improve your situation and actively strive for success, and your colleagues may appreciate your open-mindedness.

Diligence. You will need to work diligently to help shift your coworkers' perceptions of you. It is important that you demonstrate your changed work ethic by prioritizing responsibilities, completing work on time and producing consistently high quality work. Only consistency in these efforts will convince others you are making a change.

Build on it. After you start to change others perceptions, you will need to continue working to build better professional relationships. It may take time and effort to do this, since you previously let people down and you have to overcome the doubt that placed on your name. This means you will have to exercise patience and understanding as you try to rebuild your name at work.

MAKE PERMANENT CHANGES

Bad habits, sketchy friends, sloppy work habits, etc. might have contributed to your name's bad reputation, so you will need to address each of these problem areas. You can do things like stop going to bars after work, make new friends who have names that reflect what you're working toward, complete tasks at work on time, etc. Again, actions speak louder than words, or in this case your name's bad reputation.

Be authentic. Talk to people about how you're working to change the perception of your name. Ask them their opinions of what you should do. Avoid the trap of appearing overly "good" so that you don't come off as trying too hard or being disingenuous. If you seem honest in your efforts, people will be more inclined to help you, as well as think better of your name.

Take responsibility. Own your past actions and apologize. This will help to boost your integrity and make people take you seriously. Be open to feedback from others too.

Don't make excuses. Nothing turns people off more than someone trying to excuse their bad behavior. This is not taking responsibility, it's hiding from the truth. Excuses prevent you from having insights into the problems you're trying to fix.

Clear up misunderstandings. If part of the damage to your name came through lies and rumors, a public damage control campaign may be necessary. This means you will have to approach people who have been spreading the untruths about you and ask them to stop. You should also speak to people affected by the lies/rumors and express your desire to move forward. You will need to do this, since problems like this do not magically disappear. It could actually get worse if you let it go on, since people's imaginations are usually worse than reality.

Apologize. Though you might hate to admit you're wrong, doing so is a step in the right direction. Honesty and self-reflection may help you to start to repair the damage. Apologizing and asking for forgiveness is a way you can start to make things right, but an apology and a good-faith action is even better. For example, if you failed to pay back money you borrowed, apologize and then pay the person what you owe them. This will prove you're sincere and truly want to improve the situation.

Do what you say you'll do. Prove yourself to be trustworthy and competent. No one likes to be let down by someone who fails to follow through on a commitment. Let your actions speak for you.

Stop bad habits. Stop gossiping, excessive drinking, taking drugs and any other undesirable habits. You might also think about changing your social circle so you aren't tempted by friends with bad habits. Everyone is going to watch you closely to see if you're serious about changing, so be sure to do your best to leave the bad habits behind.

Stay positive. This is one of the best ways to clear the cloud of negativity that surrounds your name. Encourage others and refrain from criticizing. Do good deeds, but don't get carried away. Overcompensating isn't the way to go. Be consistent in your positive attitude without demanding acknowledgment for it, and people will start to view your name differently.

Treat people well. How you treat others is a direct reflection on your name. Be sure you treat people with basic dignity and have empathy for every person's situation. Listen to what people are telling you and consider their opinions and input. Basically, treat people they way you want them to treat you.

Reinvent yourself. Imagine yourself as the new, improved person with the highly polished name who is highly regarded everywhere you go. Think about how this person would be have, what traits are they respected for, what values do they live by, how do they perform at work, etc. and then set goals for yourself based on this imagined person.

Once you've done all the work, people will start to notice you have changed. Just be sure to keep up the work and don't think you can relax once your name has moved onto the good side of the scale.

In view of this, I also do my best to maintain always
a blameless conscience both before God and before men.

— Acts 24:16:

And he must have a good reputation with those outside the church,
so that he will not fall into reproach and the snare of the devil.

— 1 Timothy 3:7

Conclusion

The way people perceive your name is based on the sum of your actions, i.e. your character and who you are. In other words, your name is made up of anything and everything you do in your life. Successful people maintain their names religiously because they know how important it is to have a good name.

In effect, your name determines your standing in society — it's a measure of your character, integrity, honesty and influence. You name is invaluable and irreplaceable and stays with you your entire life, so make sure it reflects who you truly are and who you wish to be in the future.

About the Author

Mike Siver is a Master Addiction Counselor, Certified Domestic Violence Counselor and a Board Certified Biblical Counselor. Before retiring, he provided Anger Management, Domestic Violence, Substance Abuse counseling and assessments, and is a Chaplain for Forgotten Man Ministries. Currently is a co-facilitator for an IOP Substance Abuse and Life Skills program based on his book *Why Did I Do That?* for the local Veterans Administration.

He also facilitates a weekly program based on his book, *What Role Do I Play,* for young people transitioning from jail back into the community.

Made in the USA
Columbia, SC
17 October 2022

69601629R00065